The World Is Un~~~~~~
But That Doesn't Have T~~~~

the Eden Option

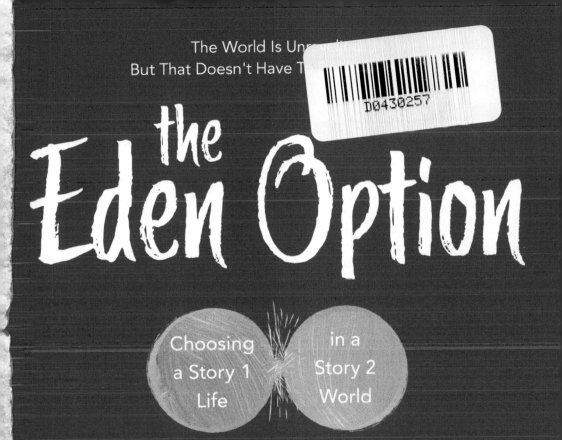

Choosing a Story 1 Life

in a Story 2 World

Allen Arnold

Author of *The Story of With*

Scripture quotations marked MSG are taken from THE MESSAGE, copyright © 1993, 2002, 2018 by Eugene H. Peterson. Used by permission of NavPress. All rights reserved. Represented by Tyndale House Publishers, a Division of Tyndale House Ministries.

Scripture quotations marked NCV are taken from the New Century Version®. Copyright © 2005 by Thomas Nelson. Used by permission. All rights reserved.

Scripture quotations marked NIV are taken from the Holy Bible, New International Version®, NIV®. Copyright © 1973, 1978, 1984, 2011 by Biblica, Inc.® Used by permission of Zondervan. All rights reserved worldwide. www.zondervan.com. The "NIV" and "New International Version" are trademarks registered in the United States Patent and Trademark Office by Biblica, Inc.®

Scripture quotations marked NKJV are taken from the New King James Version®. Copyright © 1982 by Thomas Nelson. Used by permission. All rights reserved.

Scripture quotations marked NLT are taken from the Holy Bible, New Living Translation, copyright ©1996, 2004, 2015 by Tyndale House Foundation. Used by permission of Tyndale House Publishers, a Division of Tyndale House Ministries, Carol Stream, Illinois 60188. All rights reserved.

Scripture quotations marked TLB are taken from The Living Bible copyright © 1971. Used by permission of Tyndale House Publishers, a Division of Tyndale House Ministries, Carol Stream, Illinois 60188. All rights reserved.

Scripture quotations marked TPT are from The Passion Translation®. Copyright © 2017, 2018 by Passion & Fire Ministries, Inc. Used by permission. All rights reserved. ThePassionTranslation.com.

Printed in the United States of America
ISBN: 978-0-578-31905-6 (print)

First Edition

10 9 8 7 6 5 4 3 2 1

To My Mom

Your heart and home hold such beautiful memories.

May our best stories together be the ones still ahead.

You don't think your way into a new kind of living.
You live your way into a new kind of thinking.

Henri Nouwen

Accelerating in the Wrong Direction

It isn't just your imagination. The world is accelerating.

More, it's unraveling because it was never meant to be what it's become. But it isn't just the world. The unraveling is also happening inside us.

In spite of technology that connects us all, we're growing more disconnected. Even in a crowd, we feel alone. Virtual reality takes us farther from what's real. We're somehow bored and overwhelmed. Energy drinks can't quench our exhaustion. Distractions won't fill our emptiness.

We're losing confidence in this world. And honestly, we never should have put our confidence there.

God invites us into a better story. A life of active, daily intimacy with the Creator of galaxies, oceans, and wildflowers. That was Eden. A place with God at the epicenter where Adam and Eve were fully seen, known, and loved.

I call this way of life Story 1. But experiencing it requires more than just believing in God. As James reminds us,

> Are there still some among you who hold that "only believing" is enough? . . . Well, remember that the demons believe this too—so strongly that they tremble in terror! (James 2:19 TLB)

Adam and Eve were believers in God before and after the fall. But belief alone wasn't enough to keep them in Eden . . . or in union with God. It isn't enough for us either.

I'm a believer who loves God deeply. Yet I was spending too much time in the wrong story. My hunch is that's true for most believers.

We're deeply embedded in Story 2. It's all we've ever known, so we've made it our home and learned to play by its rules. Worse, we think God does as well. But there's been a better way since the beginning. Adam and Eve didn't choose it in Eden. But we can choose it now.

The Eden Option is a roadmap to experiencing the true story we were created for. It reveals God's original design for our lives, how we lost it, and why it matters more than we imagine. When we return to Story 1, we reclaim four traits that Adam and Eve relinquished in Eden. Union. Voice. Vision. Rest. In Story 2, these four things remain lost. But in Story 1, we can actually can get them back.

Along the way, you'll find Eden Beacons. Like lighthouses, these brief thoughts and questions illuminate aspects of the original paradise . . . and signal the way towards the New Eden.

C. S. Lewis said, "If you are on the wrong road, progress means doing an about-turn and walking back to the right road; and in that case, the [one] who turns back soonest is the most progressive" (*The Case for Christianity*).

That's what we're after. The true Story God has been telling since before time began. Let's discover it together.

The question is not what we intended ourselves to be,
but what He intended us to be when He made us.

C. S. Lewis, *Mere Christianity*

Losing My Voice

The day that changed everything for me began in the most normal way. Same as every summer weekend. Doing yard work.

On this particular morning, something else was on my mind. If you had asked me what it was, I would have said . . . well, I wouldn't have said anything.

I had no voice. For going on three months.

It began when I was the only speaker for a three-day event with sessions morning to evening. The back-to-back talks took a toll on my vocal cords. After the conference ended, my normal deep voice was reduced to a hoarse whisper. Beyond the obvious inconveniences, speaking is a large part of my calling. I participate in a weekly podcast, conduct coaching sessions, and lead events. All of which require a strong, healthy voice.

Yet up until that moment, I took my voice for granted. I never gave my vocal cords a thought. I just opened my mouth and spoke. At least until three months ago.

The first month, I tried everything from silence (my kids loved that!) to voice exercises to consuming vast amounts of hot honey tea with lemon. Nothing worked. Once it was apparent this was more than just a case of temporary hoarseness, I made an appointment with an ENT (Ear, Nose, Throat) specialist.

The doctor placed a high-tech tube with a camera into my nose and guided it down my throat by remote control. As the cold, slick tube slithered down my throat, I felt like I was in a scene from the movie *Alien*. I did my best not to gag. I remained silent because, well, I had no voice. And besides, as the *Alien* movie poster declared, "In space, no one can hear you scream."

The doctor offered a comforting smile. "Just breathe normal, like always." Like people do when an alien thrusts its tentacles down their nose to invade their body. Got it.

The image on the monitor revealed two nodules on my vocal cords. The doctor explained they were like micro calluses that propped my vocal cords open and prevented air from flowing as it needed to. Turns out it's a frequent problem for speakers and singers who overstress their voices. He said until the nodules were surgically removed, my voice would remain hoarse and weak. His first available time for the procedure was months away. Two. Long. Months.

I left the room and walked down the long hall with my paperwork. I should have been relieved. I had a solid diagnosis. A plan for surgery. And the issue wasn't life-threatening. All good, right? Yet all I could muster was a sigh. I felt like I was in the wrong story ... without knowing what that even meant. But with no real voice and no perceived alternative, I shook off the feeling and headed to my truck, trying to make peace with the long, silent wait.

That was months ago. Now, as I wiped the sweat from my brow while mowing the yard, I knew the surgery was just three days away. It wouldn't be long until I had my voice back. Yet something still seemed off.

That's when God showed up ... with another option.

If we reduce the Christian faith to only that which we can explain, we end up with a paper-thin, watered-down, cheap knock-off of Christianity that no longer has the capacity to astonish.

Brian Zahnd, *Beauty Will Save the World*

Finding My Story

Covered in sweat and grass clippings, I sensed God asking me a question.

Allen, do you want Story 1 or Story 2?

The question reminded me of a game show host asking the contestant, "Do you want what's behind door #1 or door #2?"

I knew the question wasn't frivolous. But I had no idea what it meant. What's Story 1? And is Story 2 better or worse? Or was I just becoming delusional in the heat? I shut the mower off and sat on the lawn. I love questions from God. I see them as his invitation into conversation.

I asked God to tell me more about the two choices.

Over the next half hour or so, he revealed more about the options.

Story 1. Cancel the surgery. Step with God into faith and mystery regarding my voice.

Story 2. Have the scheduled procedure.

He was giving me a choice, but few details on how either would play out.

I sensed God's assurance I would one day have my voice back either way. And that something more was at play in the spiritual realm. God began to show me how the enemy's goal since Eden was to come against his voice . . . and ours.

Story 1 made me uncomfortable. Yes, God did say I'd eventually have my voice back. But he didn't say how it would happen or how long it would take. Story 2 sure seemed the most practical, expedient path. The doctor had successfully performed this procedure countless times. It was scheduled. All I had to do was show up. Story 2 seemed the more rational choice. After all, God provides healing through surgeons all the time. And the immediacy of surgery sounded a lot better than God's wait-and-see option. I'd been without a voice for such a long time.

The gravitational pull to Story 2 was intense.

But I remembered that feeling of something within me being "off" during the doctor appointment. Yes, I wanted my voice back. Desperately. But Story 2 just didn't fit me well. Like wearing pants two sizes too small. On the other hand, I couldn't quit thinking about Story 1. I wanted to read that story. Wear that story. Step into that story.

If both options were made into documentaries, which would you want to watch? One with me having routine surgery, or one where I step from the familiar to the unfamiliar with God … at his invitation?

Me too.

So I chose Story 1.

**The riddles of God
are more satisfying than
the solutions of man.**

G. K. Chesterton, *Introduction to the Book of Job*

It Will Be Awkward

The next morning, I called my throat doctor's office. Canceling just days before the procedure was uncomfortable. But the truly awkward part was explaining why. Yes, I could have just made up an excuse. But if I was going to pursue Story 1, I wanted to own it.

"So you no longer want the procedure?" his assistant asked.

"That's right. I, well, I believe God is inviting me to choose another story."

After a few seconds of chirping crickets, she noted if I changed my mind, the first opening was currently ninety days out.

As I hung up, I could feel doubt rising. Doubt about what that person thought of me. And doubt about foregoing this accepted path to fix my vocal cords. But with God's help, my resolve held. The decision was never a medical issue for me. I know God works through skilled doctors. My focus was on the adventure God was inviting me into.

No two situations will look alike. God may invite you to have a surgery, postpone a trip, or start a business. Before any big decision, especially one that impacts your family, verify what you're sensing aligns with Scripture rather than just your own desires. Ask others who walk closely with God to do listening prayer for clarity on what God is saying ... and when to act on it. That's what I did in my situation. From there, enter into Story 1 knowing the only guarantee is that God will be with you. That has to be enough. If anything becomes more important, the enemy will work overtime to cause you to doubt God's goodness.

So how did the story of my voice play out? Keeping this real, here's part of my follow-up email conversation with the throat doctor. Sending it felt risky and, yes, awkward. But I sensed God's nudge to invite him into the wonder of what happened.

"I wanted to share some amazing news with you. I canceled my surgery to cut the nodules from my vocal cords because I felt God was inviting me to another story ... one that he was doing that would exceed my wildest imagination. I definitely wanted my voice back. But even more, I wanted

to enter into the story God was offering me. One with no guarantees other than his presence. Within three days of cancelling the surgery, I had my full-strength voice back. And even after recent speaking events, it has remained full-strength. I know you hear a lot of bad news. Just wanted to share with you this story of a miraculous healing in a situation where the only cure seemed to be surgery. I'm in awe of God and his ability to exceed our best-case scenarios."

Within hours, I received his response.

"Being in medicine it gets easy to just not expect miraculous healing or to pray in such a way that you 'give God a way out' in the event healing doesn't happen. To hear a story like yours makes me want to double down and trust more fully!"

God used the temporary loss of my voice to help me find Story 1. And I was getting my first taste of both the awkwardness and the beauty of it.

Eden Beacon

Jesus in Eden

Have you ever wondered what Jesus was doing in Eden? As part of the Trinity, he was actively involved in creation. The first chapter of John tells us that all things were created in and through Jesus. Which would, of course, include Eden. And Adam and Eve. And, well, everything.

In Eden, we have the appearance of God, Adam, Eve, the serpent, animals, and cherubim (with flaming swords).

Given that Jesus had an irreplaceable role in creation and would be the cure for Adam and Eve's fall, is it plausible he wouldn't be present in Eden? In his own creation? Doubtful.

Remember, this would be the pre-incarnate Jesus. He didn't take on human form or the name Jesus until he was born to the virgin Mary.

Though we don't see Jesus in Eden, God offers this prophetic word, of which Jesus is the fulfillment:

> From now on you and the woman will be enemies, as will your offspring and hers. You will strike his heel, but he will crush your head. (Genesis 3:15 TLB)

For all the enemy's scheming, he seemed to forget that all things were created in and through Jesus...including Eden and himself. Though the enemy led Adam and Eve into the wrong story, Jesus was the one true Story in which everything finds its deeper meaning. And at great cost, he would prevail. Listen to how the great lion Aslan touches on this theme in *The Lion, the Witch and the Wardrobe*, by C. S. Lewis:

> Though the Witch knew the Deep Magic, there is a magic deeper still which she did not know. Her knowledge goes back only to the dawn of time. But if she could have looked a little further back, into the stillness and the darkness before Time dawned, she would have read there a different incantation. She would have known that when a willing victim who had committed no treachery was killed in a traitor's stead, the Table would crack and Death itself would start working backward.

How might Jesus have filled his days and evenings in Eden? It's a question that stirs my heart with wonder. May it do the same for you.

When the whole world is running towards a cliff, he who is running in the opposite direction appears to have lost his mind.

C. S. Lewis

Invisible Force Field

After months of not having much of a voice, its return was hard to miss.

But it was the reaction of others that caught me off guard. Especially after the amazing response from my doctor.

For the most part, the people I shared my story with believed in God. Yet few expressed awe, asked questions, or wanted to engage in the topic. After a polite nod, raised eyebrow, or moment of awkward silence, they usually shifted the conversation to the weather or the weekend football game. I was hitting an invisible force field of some kind. I was puzzled at first but think I know why now.

Over time, we accept the story we find ourselves in as normal operating procedure. So we no longer see what's really going on. Like the best Agatha Christie mysteries, the clues are right in front of us, but we miss them because our upfront assumptions about the story we're in lead us to the wrong conclusions.

When something pushes up against this false narrative, we tend to push back or disengage. Because it doesn't fit our perceptions of how life—or God—works. One of the signs this is true is how we've reduced stories of men and women in the Bible to one-dimensional morality lessons rather than examples of the way we can live. We still believe in God but view him as distant so we get on with life. The roots of this run really deep. All the way back to creation. More on that soon.

For now, realize that any resistance you may be feeling is like the invisible force field I was bumping into. The enemy doesn't want us embracing a story that draws us into greater intimacy with God. Which is exactly what Story 1 does. So he'll throw any distraction he can at us to keep us in Story 2.

If that fails and we enter into Story 1, he'll do his best to make us doubt our decision. But the deeper doubt centers on God's goodness. Will we let go of our unreliable banner of certainty and trust God with a wilder, riskier, less controllable story?

This is where the reaction of others comes into play. Some may respond in beautifully encouraging ways. Like my throat doctor did. But others may stare blankly or try to prove why we're foolish or naïve for living this way. That's okay. The goal isn't to persuade or convince others but to simply share the wonder and the awkwardness of our choice.

The Story 1 life isn't a nice addition to our current life. It is an entirely new way of seeing God, ourselves, and this world.

It is seeking God's active involvement in the rhythm of our days, dreams, and challenges. It is knowing we are never alone. He is at the epicenter of everything we do, and we keep our eyes on him rather than the world for how to live, work, create, rest, and love.

The institutions rooted in Story 2—whether political, business, educational, entertainment, or even religious—will never support those breaking free into Story 1. In many cases, they will actively oppose it. Don't let such resistance cause you to doubt this journey.

Before we get ahead of ourselves, let's slow down to learn more about the differences between Story 1 and Story 2.

Story 1 is the original, true story
we were made for.
A way of life with
God at the epicenter.

Story 2 is the default narrative we're born into.
It tries to make life work without
God's active, intimate presence.

A Tale of Two Stories

So what are the key differences between the two Stories? Here's a quick overview.

In Story 1, God is at the epicenter. In Story 2, we put ourselves at the center.

In both cases, everything flows from there. For good or for ill.

For greater clarity, let's compare their key traits.

In Story 1, we live in intimacy with God as sons and daughters. We awake with childlike expectancy. This relationship leads to rest and restoration. Infinite possibilities and wonder run through the DNA of Story 1. It is filled with God's presence.

Story 1	Story 2
God at the Center	You're at the Center
Faith & Hope	Doubt & Despair
Seen & Known	Unseen & Unknown
Loved for Who You Are	Loved for What You Do
A Father Who Provides	You Rely on Yourself
Anything Is Possible	Limited Options
Heart is Awake & Alive	Heart is Numb & Shut-Down
Living from Restoration	Looking for Relief
Open-Handed Abundance	Closed-Handed Scarcity
Love-Based Decisions	Fear-Based Decisions
Imagination for What Could Be	Indoctrination for What Must Be
Wisdom and Faith	Knowledge and Facts
Expectancy	Expectations
Freedom	Control
Wonder	Boredom
Present	Distracted

In Story 2, we settle for a world in which God is largely off-stage. We toss and turn with unmet expectations, seeking relief but settling for addictions. Limited possibilities are the norm in Story 2. We accuse God of being distant as we distance ourselves from him. Though over time, the Story 2 life feels normal to us, it's not what we were made for. It's just what we're used to.

In Story 1, we have dialogues with God and others, asking questions and listening. In Story 2, we have monologues with God and others, stating what we think and want. Story 1 permeates our thoughts, hopes, and dreams. We're drawn to movies and songs and art that reflects the themes and perspectives of Story 1—while losing interest in those that embrace Story 2. You realize independence from God—the hallmark of a Story 2 life—only leads to greater isolation. While Story 1 dependence on God leads to greater intimacy.

If you're not sure which story you're in, you're almost certainly in Story 2. Why? Because it's the default narrative. We're born into Story 2 but can be reborn into Story 1. But we have to actively choose that. You'd remember if you had. Based on these traits, which most describes your current world? More importantly, which story would you like to be yours?

We spend our days either
believing life is up to us
or experiencing the wildness
of life with God.
You choose which reality to call home.

No Neutral Ground

In his Gospel, Luke describes the collision of these two stories—as well as the stakes involved.

> If you grasp and cling to life on your terms, you'll lose it, but if you let that life go, you'll get life on God's terms. (Luke 17:33 MSG)

In a world that's conditioned us to expect endless options, Luke boils it down to two choices.

We can't opt out, create new options, or remain neutral. Nor should we.

As C. S. Lewis says, "There is no neutral ground in the universe. Every square inch, every split second is claimed by God, and counterclaimed by Satan" (*Christian Reflections*).

We don't live in a world of neutrality but rather one of two competing narratives.

There is God's story and there is the counter story.

What's confusing is when the choices before us don't appear to be opposites. Often it seems to be just a slight difference or twist. So we compromise, not realizing the way our choices ripple beyond us.

Story 1 has been under attack for every generation since Eden. Because God has an enemy and so do we. The role of the enemy in these two stories will become clearer soon. For now, just know the tension between these two stories isn't theoretical or poetic.

It's impossible to simultaneously live two stories. Only one can be your home base. And the more you understand the toxicity of Story 2, the less time you'll want to spend in that broken world.

We have all read...the story of the man
who has forgotten his name. This man walks about
the streets and can see and appreciate everything;
only he cannot remember who he is.
Well, every man is that man in the story.
Every man has forgotten who he is ...
We are all under the same mental calamity;
we have all forgotten our names.
We have all forgotten what we really are.

G. K. Chesterton, *Orthodoxy*

Secret Sauce of Story 1

We are eternal beings. After this life, our life continues. But only one story continues in the coming kingdom. Story 1.

Only it offers a way of life that we can live both now . . . and continue living in the coming kingdom. That's because it reflects an Eden view of life, with God at the epicenter.

The life of Enoch provides a dramatic example of this way of living. He spent his life walking in close fellowship with God. Then he disappeared from this world without dying. God simply took him (Genesis 5:23–24). He went from living Story 1 here to living Story 1 in the kingdom . . . without missing a beat.

When we choose Story 1, we begin to experience the power of faith, hope, and love now. And our lives become infused with three things that last forever.

> Three things will last forever—faith, hope, and love—and the great-est of these is love. (1 Corinthians 13:13 NLT)

Of the three traits, love is the greatest. It's the secret sauce of Story 1.

We intuitively know this. Almost every movie, song, or speech gains its strength by tapping into the power of love, faith, and hope. It's just the object of those traits where things get messy. Faith in what? Hope in what? Love of what? We tend to focus our faith, hope, and love on cre-ated things rather than the Creator.

When that happens, we become tangled in the trappings of a Story 2 life. But when we love God above all else, we increase the likelihood of staying in Story 1. That's why the greatest commandment is this:

> Love the Lord your God with all your heart and with all your soul and with all your mind and with all your strength. (Mark 12:30 NIV)

It's also why love is even more powerful than belief. Had Adam and Eve loved God with all their hearts, doubt would have found no home. And Eden would have remained their home.

We walk by faith and not by sight because there are places to go that cannot be seen and the scope of our vision is too small for our strides.

Rich Mullins, *Winds of Heaven, Stuff of Earth*

Steep Your Life in God-Reality

Our world is moving more virtual every day.

Most spend more time staring at screens than interacting with real people … or real life. Many reading this will even challenge what real means anymore. That's how comfortable we've come to be with the artificial.

And when we move against it, we're often told to "get real" and accept the ways of this world. But that's actually just the opposite of what's needed.

One of the many benefits of choosing a Story 1 life is the return to what is real. Not what we say or feel is real, but reality as God made it to be.

Think of it this way. God has always existed. He created everything that is. Everything we call reality was made by One who is far more real than it is.

So in a world of competing realities, nothing is more real than God. Which means the further we get from God, the shakier our foundation becomes.

And like a beacon, Scripture calls us back to God-reality.

> Steep your life in God-reality, God-initiative, God-provisions. Don't worry about missing out. You'll find all your everyday human concerns will be met. Give your entire attention to what God is doing right now, and don't get worked up about what may or may not happen tomorrow. (Matthew 6:33–34 MSG)

How did we lose this original God-steeped Story? Where did it go? Or more honestly, where did we go?

It's called Story 1 because it reflects our origin story in Eden. Let's revisit paradise and see it with new eyes to better understand what we had, why it was lost, and how to get it back.

Eden is at the epicenter of everything.
It is the first and truest glimpse
of what reality
is meant to be.

Answers
in Eden

Origin Amnesia

We love origin scenes in movies. They help us understand how things began and why characters behave the way they do. It gives us empathy … and orientation.

Yet the recollection of our own origin story is spotty at best. Especially when it comes to Eden. Like a collective shockwave of amnesia, the enemy has muddied our memory of the life and home we were created for.

When people do talk about Eden, they jump straight from creation to the fall. Doing so completely skips over the tender beginning of Adam and Eve's* story with God.

And it keeps us in Story 2. Because we can't turn our eyes to what we no longer remember.

....

*Though chronologically, Adam gave Eve her name *after* the fall (Genesis 3:20), I'm using it throughout this book rather than call her "the woman" until after they lose Eden.

But Eden is worth remembering. The name Eden means delight or paradise. It was a place of lush abundance. Unspoiled beauty. Peace and tranquility. Unexplored mysteries. There was ample time for everything. And no self-consciousness, anxiety, or loss. Adam and Eve walked with God in the cool of the garden. They were new creatures within a new creation that revolved around its Creator.

God didn't just create the first man and woman. He fathered them. Those are the first two ways God reveals himself in Scripture. As Creator and Father.

We know the story of God having Adam name the animals. But before that, who did you think taught Adam and Eve language? Who else would have explained the mysteries and wonder of the new creation? Or the story of their story?

Who knows how long this season lasted? It likely wasn't a rushed process but one of spaciousness, kindness, love, and patience. The modern human cycle of life and death hadn't yet begun. Remember, Adam wasn't born in a womb. God breathed life into the dirt of the ground and Adam awoke as an adult male, not a newborn infant. There was no pregnancy. No umbilical cord (or, presumably, belly button).

Though we're far from Eden today, we have access to this same relational intimacy with God.

> I will be your Father, and you will be my sons and daughters.
> (2 Corinthians 6:18 NLT)

As Creator and Father, God invites us to co-create with him as his sons and daughters. Not just once upon a time. But today. Now. Though it may be hard to believe, God is less interested in what you do for him than in whether you enter into life with him.

> Doing things for God is the opposite of entering into what God does for you. (Galatians 3:11–12 MSG)

Our life isn't primarily about doing things for God. It is about experiencing our story actively and intimately with God. Just as it was for Adam and Eve.

The earliest vision their eyes beheld was not one another. Upon humanity's awakening, they first saw the glad smile of God.

Cara L. T. Murphy, *The Inquisitive Christ*

Eden Beacon

Human. Life.

The name *Adam* stands for "red earth" or "human."

The name *Eve* means "life."

Taken together, my friend Nicole notes, the names Adam and Eve represent "Human Life."

How cool is that? And how sad their choice was for the future of humanity. They believed the Tree of Knowledge would make them more like God. Instead, it moved them further from God and from the life God had created them for.

Human Life.

Jesus came to redeem it along with everything else lost in Eden. Scripture refers to him in multiple places as the new Adam. As I spent time considering this Eden-based designation for Jesus, it led me to wonder.

Does something or someone represent the new Eve? I honestly have no idea. But it's my favorite kind of question. One that draws me to God and Scripture to explore further in humility and wonder.

The Reality of Eden

If the enemy can't keep us from remembering Eden, he prefers that we not see it as a real place.

There's only one problem with that. It isn't the view found in Scripture.

Jesus is referred to as the second Adam. If Adam were a made-up character, that would be a bit like your neighbor being called the second Edmund from Narnia, who came to set right all Edmund's wrongs.

> Adam, the first man, was made from the dust of the earth, while Christ, the second man, came from heaven. (1 Corinthians 15:47 NLT)

But there is a great difference between Adam's sin and God's gracious gift. For the sin of this one man, Adam, brought death to many. But even greater is God's wonderful grace and his gift of forgiveness to many through this other man, Jesus Christ. . . Yes, Adam's one sin brings condemnation for everyone, but Christ's one act of righteousness brings a right relationship with God and new life for everyone. (Romans 5:15, 18 NLT)

Then there's the genealogy of Jesus. Scripture records the lineage from Adam to Jesus. If Adam isn't real, at what point does the genealogy get real?

Enoch, who lived in the seventh generation after Adam ...
(Jude 1:16 NLT)

Paul also addressed a period of time from Adam to Moses. So either both were real or you have to assume Moses didn't exist either.

Still, everyone died—from the time of Adam to the time of Moses—even those who did not disobey an explicit commandment of God, as Adam did. Now Adam is a symbol, a representation of Christ, who was yet to come. (Romans 5:14 NLT)

Timothy clearly believed in the literal story of what happened in Eden.

And it was not Adam who was fooled by Satan, but Eve, and sin was the result. (1 Timothy 2:14 NLT)

In Eden death entered through the sin of one man and one woman (Romans 5:12). God promised it would be through the woman's seed (Jesus) that the enemy's head would be crushed (Genesis 3:15). If there's no Eden and no Adam and Eve, then there's no original sin and no reason for Jesus to crush the serpent's head and sacrifice himself to redeem all that was lost. The story of the crucifixion and resurrection of Jesus is ultimately connected to Eden.

That's why it's essential to address the reality of Eden. There's an equally real New Eden coming. But for now, let's see what happened in the garden with new eyes.

Middle of the Garden

The center of something is always important. It's where the important things go down. It's, as the Broadway play *Hamilton* puts it, "the room where it happens." The middle of Eden's garden was where one of the central moments in history would happen.

> Then the LORD God planted a garden in Eden in the east, and there he placed the man he had made. The LORD God made all sorts of trees grow up from the ground—trees that were beautiful and that produced delicious fruit. In the middle of the garden he placed the tree of life and the tree of the knowledge of good and evil. (Genesis 2:8–9 NLT)

God placed two trees in the center of the garden. And then he placed man in the garden to care for it, with an upfront warning.

The LORD God placed the man in the Garden of Eden to tend and watch over it. But the LORD God warned him, "You may freely eat the fruit of every tree in the garden—except the tree of the knowledge of good and evil. If you eat its fruit, you are sure to die." (Genesis 2:15–17 NLT)

The Tree of Knowledge didn't offer life. Or wisdom. Though we often mistake knowledge for wisdom.

Wisdom is a tree of life to those who eat her fruit; happy is the man who keeps on eating it. The Lord's wisdom founded the earth; his understanding established all the universe and space. (Proverbs 3:18–19 TLB)

Adam and Eve could eat freely from every other tree in the garden. They had immense freedom. Actually, total freedom . . . because they could choose the wrong tree. They just didn't have freedom from the consequences of their choice. None of us do.

Their choice was incredibly important. And it took place in the middle of the garden.

**To walk out of his will
is to walk into nowhere.**

C. S. Lewis, *Perelandra*

The Danger of Doubt

Up until this point in Eden, there was only one story. The true story.

But the serpent would challenge that story with a conversation that introduced another way to interpret life and God. It would begin the unraveling of Story 1.

> Now the serpent was more crafty than any of the wild animals the LORD God had made. He said to the woman, "Did God really say, 'You must not eat from any tree in the garden'?" The woman said to the serpent, "We may eat fruit from the trees in the garden, but God did say, 'You must not eat fruit from the tree that is in the middle of the garden, and you must not touch it, or you will die.'" "You will not certainly die," the serpent said to the woman. "For God knows that when you eat from it your eyes will be opened, and you will be like God, knowing good and evil." (Genesis 3:1–5 NIV)

Notice the language of the serpent's temptation. "Did God really say...? Surely you won't die." His words focused on loopholes and information rather than love, trust, and intimacy. His goal wasn't to stop Adam and Eve from believing in God. Just to believe that other things offered a better life.

The enemy initiated a knowledge-based conversation with Eve, using the logic of that tree, to draw her to it. He perceived being like God to be based solely in knowledge and power. Which revealed he never understood the true heart of God. What he was after was doubt. But not just any doubt. He didn't want Adam and Eve to doubt their own desires or his false narrative. He wanted them to doubt God's goodness.

Author John Eldredge put it this way:

> Satan came into the Garden and whispered to Adam and Eve—and in them, to all of us—"You cannot trust the heart of God ... he's holding out on you ... you've got to take matters under your control." He sowed the seed of mistrust in our hearts; he tempted us to seize control. It's the same lie he is using in your life today, by the way: Trusting God is way too risky. You're far too vulnerable.

Rewrite the Story. Give yourself a better part. Arrange for your own happiness. Disregard him. (*Epic: The Story God Is Telling*)

The enemy's strategy of doubt didn't end in Eden. We wrestle with it today. But doubt in God is neither necessary nor noble. David, through the Psalms, modeled a better way to handle doubt. He doubted the motive of others. The fairness of the world. The outcome of his current situation. But unlike Adam and Eve—and often us—he didn't doubt God's goodness. He wrestled through his emotions and questions about God ... *with* God. He wailed and pleaded and ranted to God. But he stayed with God through it all.

We can do the same with our disappointments. No matter what we face, it's our choice whether to remain steadfast in believing that God is real and good and present. No matter how hard it is, that's always the next, best step.

Because it's a step toward—not away from—God.

What is the real evil in this question
[*Did God really say*]?
… It is that this question already contains the
wrong answer. It is that with this question
the basic attitude of the creature toward
the Creator comes under attack. It requires
humankind to sit in judgment on God's word
instead of simply listening to it and doing it.

Dietrich Bonhoeffer, *Creation and Fall*

Eden Beacon

Why Didn't God Warn Adam?

Have you ever wondered why God didn't give Adam a heads-up of the serpent's plan? It could've saved Eve and him—and the rest of humanity—from a lot of pain and trauma.

Listen to John Eldredge's take on this pivotal moment:

Before the moment of Adam's greatest trial God provided no step-by-step plan, gave no formula for how he was to handle the whole mess. That was not abandonment; that was the way God honored Adam. *You are a man; you don't need me to hold you by the hand through this. You have what it takes.* What God *did* offer Adam was friendship. He wasn't left alone to face life; he walked with God in the cool of the day, and there they talked about love and marriage and creativity, what lessons he was learning and what adventures were to come. This is what God is offering to us as well. (*Wild at Heart*)

Perhaps you have a different theory about this. That's okay. But it's essential we see the event through the lens of God as a good Father. He created Adam and Eve to do life with them. And he gave them the honor of choosing whether to reciprocate.

He does the same for us.

We want to be God. But what kind of God? Like Lucifer? Full of earthly power and grandeur, able to wave wands and work magic, reaching out greedily for this world?

That is the god that Jesus rejected when the Holy Spirit led him into the wilderness to be tempted. And so he went not to a royal, temporal throne, but to the cross.

Adam and Eve did not live long enough to understand that the cross is the gateway to heaven. Most of us don't understand that, either, and so, like Adam and Eve, we bicker, we quarrel, we alibi, we jostle for power and glory.

Madeleine L'Engle, *And It Was Good*

What Was Lost in Eden

Adam and Eve traded the Tree of Life for the Tree of Knowledge. It was a bad trade.

What was going through Eve's mind when she made that fateful choice? We don't have to wonder.

> When the woman saw that the fruit of the tree was good for food and pleasing to the eye, and also desirable for gaining wisdom, she took some and ate it. She also gave some to her husband, who was with her, and he ate it. (Genesis 3:6 NIV)

The appeal was to their eyes, mouth, and mind—the same temptations we face today.

For all that is in the world—the lust of the flesh, the lust of the eyes, and the pride of life—is not of the Father but is of the world. (1 John 2:16 NKJV)

After listening to the wrong voice and believing the wrong story, they feasted from the wrong tree. This is the moment when Story 1 was lost and Story 2 began. Through their sin, death entered the world. Because of their choice, Adam and Eve lost four essential things.

First, they lost union with God. Doubting God didn't make them like gods. It caused them to hide from God in shame. Dietrich Bonhoeffer described the moment when God asks Adam why he is hiding like this:

He confesses his sin, but in the very act of confessing it he seeks to flee again. You gave me the woman, not I; I am not guilty, you are guilty ... So instead of standing before God, Adam falls back on the trick learned from the serpent of correcting what is in God's mind, of appealing from God the Creator to a better god, a different god ... Adam keeps on falling. The fall drops with increasing speed for an immeasurable distance. (*Creation and Fall*)

Second, they lost their voice. Adam failed to speak during Eve's temptation. Then after the fall, Adam used his voice to blame Eve. She used her voice to blame the serpent. Scripture tells us Adam lived 930 years. We don't know how long Eve lived. But from that point forward, their story goes silent.

Third, they lost their vision. The serpent promised their eyes would be opened. And they were. But not in the way they hoped.

> At that moment their eyes were opened, and they suddenly felt shame at their nakedness. So they sewed fig leaves together to cover themselves. (Genesis 3:7 NLT)

Finally, they lost the ability to rest. Their curse included pain, striving, and restlessness.

Union. Voice. Vision. Rest. In Story 2, these four things remain lost. But in Story 1, we can actually get them back.

Truth is eternal.
Knowledge is changeable.
It is disastrous to confuse them.

Madeleine L'Engle, *An Acceptable Time*

When Trees Become Towers

Adam and Eve's tragic choice didn't just affect them.

The consequences of their decision unfurled swiftly. By the time we reach the story of Noah, humanity had almost imploded. No one was living Story 1 except Noah and his family. Humanity's heart was filled with only evil. God's heart was filled with pain. He was sorry he ever made humans.

> The LORD observed the extent of human wickedness on the earth, and he saw that everything they thought or imagined was consistently and totally evil. So the LORD was sorry he had ever made them and put them on the earth. It broke his heart. (Genesis 6:5–6 NLT)

In many ways, our modern world is no different. It too has lost Story 1. Notice how Jesus ties the days of Noah to the coming end days.

> As it was in the days of Noah, so it will be at the coming of the Son of Man. For in the days before the flood, people were eating and drinking, marrying and giving in marriage, up to the day Noah entered the ark; and they knew nothing about what would happen until the flood came and took them all away. That is how it will be at the coming of the Son of Man. (Matthew 24:37–39 NIV)

Later in Genesis, we encounter the Tower of Babel. This manmade structure was surely inspired by the Tree of Knowledge. The descendants of Adam and Eve never lost their urge to be like gods.

Here's how Scripture describes it:

> At that time all mankind spoke a single language. As the population grew and spread eastward, a plain was discovered in the land of Babylon and was soon thickly populated. The people who lived there began to talk about building a great city, with a temple-tower reaching to the skies—a proud, eternal monument to themselves. (Genesis 11:1–4 TLB)

The entire project focused on the human worship of knowledge and self-achievement that excludes God. The monument wasn't just a tower but a temple being built into the heavens. The intent wasn't to worship God but to invade his space. And the root of it began with choosing Eden's forbidden tree.

The Tree of Knowledge promises power through a cold, hard infusion of information and facts. But this kind of knowing doesn't lead to greater intimacy with God. Only the Tree of Life can do that. But rather than answer all our questions, it fills us with God's presence.

If there's any doubt where the Tree of Knowledge leads, let's turn our eyes from Eden to Ecclesiastes.

Don't it always seem to go
that you don't know what you've got
'til it's gone.
They paved paradise.
Put up a parking lot.

Joni Mitchell, "Big Yellow Taxi"

A Minus That Won't Add Up

The world of Ecclesiastes isn't pretty. It was never meant to be our home.

The author of this Old Testament book was the wisest man of his world—Solomon, son of King David. And even he couldn't figure out how to make the Story 2 world he inherited work.

> These are the words of the Quester, David's son and king in Jerusalem: Smoke, nothing but smoke. There's nothing to anything—it's all smoke. What's there to show for a lifetime of work, a lifetime of working your fingers to the bone?

One generation goes its way, the next one arrives, but nothing changes ...

Everything's boring, utterly boring—no one can find any meaning in it. Boring to the eye, boring to the ear. What was will be again, what happened will happen again.

There's nothing new on this earth. Year after year it's the same old thing. Does someone call out, "Hey, *this* is new"? Don't get excited—it's the same old story. Nobody remembers what happened yesterday. And the things that will happen tomorrow? Nobody'll remember them either. Don't count on being remembered ...

Life's a corkscrew that can't be straightened, a minus that won't add up ...

Much learning earns you much trouble. The more you know, the more you hurt. (Ecclesiastes 1:1–18 MSG)

There's nothing to anything.

A corkscrew that can't be straightened.

A minus that won't add up.

The more you know, the more you hurt.

So much for the promises of the Tree of Knowledge.

By this point in our journey, you can identify all the signs of Story 2 in Ecclesiastes. It's a story of meaninglessness, confusion, boredom, and the limits of knowledge.

A recurring theme of Ecclesiastes is that "there is nothing new under the sun" (1:9 NIV). But God isn't limited to what's under the sun. With God in the story, there are no limitations. He promises to make all things new.

But only if we join God in the story he is in. Story 1.

For a time is coming when people will no longer listen to sound and wholesome teaching. They will follow their own desires and will look for teachers who will tell them whatever their itching ears want to hear. They will reject the truth and chase after myths.

2 Timothy 4:3-4 NLT

You gave me all your love,
I love making war
Chaos, she politely knocked
so I opened the door.
I looked from left to right
for somebody to blame.
I believed the viper
and I grew a pair of fangs.

The Arcadian Wild, *Principium*, "III. Fall:War"

Eden Beacon

Opposing Cherubim

We've talked a lot about Adam and Eve's choice. Angels made a choice too.

There was a war in heaven—and neutrality wasn't an option. One third of the created angelic beings chose another created being, Lucifer, over the Creator. In the process, they traded the truth for a lie.

Adam and Eve did the same. As have those who live in Story 2.

> They traded the truth about God for a lie. So they worshipped and served the things God created instead of the Creator himself ... (Romans 1:25 NLT)

It's fascinating how, after the fall, God appointed cherubim to watch over the Tree of Life. Cherubim were part of an elite, high-ranking group of angelic beings. The enemy had once been part of that group, supposedly one of the more powerful ones. Yet now cherubim who didn't side with the enemy in the heavenly war against God received a key role in Eden. With flaming swords, they blocked Adam and Eve, and presumably the enemy, from accessing the Tree of Life.

That's what appears to be at play here. Loyal cherubim protecting the Tree of Life from the defector cherub's attempt to lead yet another coup against God. This one not in heaven, but in Eden.

What the
Cheshire Cat Knew

Alice in Wonderland is a fantastical adventure story.

But Alice wouldn't serve us well as a travel guide. She's full of curiosity, but not so great at choosing between options. As her conversation with the Cheshire Cat makes obvious, she doesn't really care where she is going. She just wants to get somewhere.

> *"Would you tell me, please, which way I ought to go from here?"*

> *"That depends a good deal on where you want to get to," said the Cat.*

> *"I don't much care where—" said Alice.*

"Then it doesn't matter which way you go," said the Cat.

"—so long as I get SOMEWHERE," Alice added as an explanation.

"Oh, you're sure to do that," said the Cat, "if you only walk long enough."

The Cheshire Cat knew Alice's problem wasn't in getting somewhere. It was in not knowing where she wanted to go. It proved a poor strategy for Alice. She almost lost her head along the way. Humanity hasn't fared any better.

By choosing the wrong tree, Adam and Eve got somewhere too. And we're still trying to escape from that misguided journey.

To do so, we need to remember what we were created for and set our gaze toward that destination. Not the original Eden. But the original way of life as God meant it. I find it helpful to remember that Eden didn't leave us. We left it. But Adam and Eve didn't end Eden. They just ended their participation in it.

Later generations forgot there ever was an Eden, or doubted it ever existed. So we just keep walking. Not sure where we're going but frantically trying to get there.

Like Alice, we'll achieve that minimal goal. Story 2 is full of such wanderers. But the answer isn't to keep walking, content to get "somewhere." The sobering reality is we can spend our entire lives walking through Story 2 and remain stuck in it.

Or we can awaken to the choice at hand. The option of Story 1.

That journey is possible, but it requires us to live by choice rather than chance.

Keep It Simple

We live in a culture of seemingly unlimited choices. We're conditioned to think more options are better. Anything less feels restricting.

In 1909, Henry Ford, the founder of the Ford Motor Company, famously made this disruptive announcement to streamline manufacturing time and costs: "Any customer can have a car painted any color that he wants so long as it is black" (*My Life and Work*).

Our minds can hardly fathom such a limiting perspective. One choice really is no choice. Yet many options aren't always helpful either. Consider the sociological experiment done in a grocery store in Menlo Park, California. It involved an in-store display that rotated between six and twenty-four kinds of jam. The results were striking. Customers with fewer options were ten times more likely to purchase than those with too many choices. In his book *The Paradox of Choice*, psychologist Barry Schwartz says this experiment reveals the downside of too many choices.

Too many options, it turns out, is too much.

The journey with God isn't supposed to be complex or complicated. Yet Story 2 takes us in the opposite direction. The native language of the enemy is lies (John 8:44). But, as Mark Twain noted, being honest simplifies life: "If you tell the truth, you don't have to remember anything."

The macro choice to live a Story 1 life leads to a story where every other micro choice makes more sense than the randomness of Story 2. Yet we push against simple. Paul explains the danger of this tendency by connecting it to Eden.

> But I am frightened, fearing that in some way you will be led away from your pure and simple devotion to our Lord, just as Eve was deceived by Satan in the Garden of Eden. (2 Corinthians 11:3 TLB)

When the Roman captain trusted Jesus to heal his servant from a distance rather than in person, Jesus was astonished. Don't miss why.

> Taken aback, Jesus said, "I've yet to come across this kind of simple trust …." (Matthew 8:10 MSG)

The Sermon on the Mount is one of the most famous speeches in history. In it, Jesus stunned listeners with a new way to see the world and themselves. The power of the message was in making complex issues simple. He concluded this epic message with four simple parables. Though each is unique, they all reinforce the same theme: we live in a world of two opposing choices.

He revealed this through stories of two paths, two trees, two ways to pursue God, and two homes. Do yourself a favor and read the full parables in Matthew 7:13–26. Using our language, each provides a Story 1 and Story 2 option ... and reveals the consequences.

How did the crowd respond to these cautionary parables? Did they feel like Jesus was limiting their options? Not at all. They were astonished at how simple he made it.

> And so it was, when Jesus had ended these sayings, that the people were astonished at His teaching. (Matthew 7:28 NKJV)

Don't make it complicated. You have two choices. But they sure aren't equal. Once you look for it, you'll find the pattern of dual options everywhere in Scripture.

A Glimpse Is All It Takes

How do we escape Ecclesiastes so we can start to experience aspects of Eden in our lives?

We can't go back in time. We won't physically find the Eden of creation . . . though many explorers have tried. But we can do something even better. Begin a homeward journey to the New Eden.

This is what the great women and men of the Bible did. They kept their eyes and their hearts focused on their true home. Because even though it was still far away, they knew it was an exponentially better country than anything this Story 2 world has to offer.

> People who live this way make it plain that they are looking for their true home. If they were homesick for the old country, they could have gone back any time they wanted. But they were after a far better country than that—*heaven* country. You can see why God is so proud of them, and has a City waiting for them. (Hebrews 11:14–16 MSG)

That City is waiting not just for them. It's waiting for us as well.

It is the New Eden. With God at the epicenter. And us at home.

Along any journey, it's normal to lose hope at times. In those moments, a glimpse is all it takes to remind us of what awaits.

I experienced the power of such a glimpse recently. My favorite place is the ocean. The blue-green color of the water and salty scent of the sea awaken my senses. The rhythmic waves and playful breeze calm my soul. I love standing on the shore and taking in the same view of sky and water that's been on display since time began.

But the closest I had been to the beach the past six years was the ocean painting in my office. So when my family and I headed to Florida this past summer, I was filled with anticipation. We arrived a little before sunset and headed to a restaurant near the shore. We put our name on the waitlist, grabbed a buzzer, and headed to the beach.

As I crossed the street and the ocean came into view, I was speechless. My wife and kids ran across the sand into the water. I just stood and tried to take it all in. I'd waited so many years for this exact moment. Until it was abruptly disrupted by the flashing, pulsating buzzer in my hand. Our table was ready. Way early.

I reluctantly turned from the ocean, knowing it would be the next day before I could fully experience the beach. I was momentarily disheartened. After all those years, all I got was a glimpse.

Yet that was all it took to awaken my desire. I was suddenly good, knowing what awaited me. I hope this book evokes the same feeling within you. Not for the beach. But for the New Eden.

Alice may still not know where she's headed, but we do. Let's begin our Homeward Journey now.

Psycho-babble is that language spoken by sailors who have become so interested in navigating their way around their boat that they have forgotten to read the stars and the sea.

Rich Mullins, Thoughts and Reflections from The World as Best as I Remember It

The
Homeward
Journey

I think everyone is just trying to get home.

Charlie Mackesy,
The Boy, the Mole, the Fox and the Horse

Looking for Home

Have you noticed how in almost every great story, the protagonist is on a search for home? These stories resonate on such a deep level because we too are looking for home.

The original Eden home was created by God and filled with his presence. He walked with Adam and Eve in the cool of the day. There was an expectancy for each new adventure and discovery. It was filled with an atmosphere of love rather than fear.

But when Adam and Eve chose the Tree of Knowledge over the Tree of Life, intimacy was traded for independence. As C. S. Lewis stated in a lecture he gave on Milton's classic work on the fall: "*Paradise Lost* records a real, irreversible, unrepeatable process . . . the great change in every individual soul from happy dependence to miserable self-assertion . . ." (Preface to *Paradise Lost*, 1942 edition).

Adam and Eve were interested in what the Tree of Knowledge could do for them, not for how it would help them more fully know God or each other. Rather than lead to a better home, they found themselves with less of everything that really mattered. They were home-less.

My counselor is almost eighty years old. He is one of the wisest, kindest, and most alive humans I've ever spent time with. During his more than fifty years of counseling thousands, he has seen it all. And he recently told me he's certain that the deepest desire of every person is to be fully seen, known, and loved. Most don't believe this longing will ever be met. Because if anyone ever fully knew their most secret thoughts, they couldn't be fully loved.

Yet deep within us, the hope remains of finding a home where this is true.

Hiraeth is a Welsh word that can't be described by a single English word. It conveys a yearning for a home that we can't return to, no longer exists, or perhaps never was. It's not just looking for a home. It's a longing for our true home.

This is what our hearts ache for. A home, to use C. S. Lewis's phrase, "of happy dependence." One with God at the epicenter where we are fully seen, known, and loved.

The goal isn't to return to the original Eden. We're setting our sights on the New Eden. We're going forward—not backward. Though we won't arrive in the New Eden until the coming kingdom, we can experience key aspects of it now.

Choosing the Eden Option is the way to get there. The Homeward Journey is how we pursue it.

Eden Beacon
God Had a Choice

After Adam and Eve chose to doubt and disobey God, he could have ended the human story right there. But he didn't. He chose us even when we didn't choose him.

> You didn't choose me. I chose you. (John 15:16 NLT)

The story God is telling has always been a love story. And because of that, he didn't have to make that choice after Adam and Eve's betrayal in Eden. He made it before the creation of the world.

> For he chose us in him before the creation of the world to be holy and blameless in his sight. In love, he predestined us for adoption to sonship through Jesus Christ, in accordance with his pleasure and will. (Ephesians 1:4–5 NIV)

But it gets even better. God didn't just choose us. He doesn't just help us in this Homeward Journey.

He *is* our home.

> Lord, you have been our home since the beginning. Before the
> mountains were born and before you created the earth and the
> world, you are God. You have always been, and you will always be.
> (Psalm 90:1–2 NCV)

As pastor and theologian Eugene Peterson phrases this same
passage,

> God, it seems you've been our home forever; long
> before the mountains were born, long before you
> brought earth itself to birth, from "once upon a
> time" to "kingdom come"—you are God.
> (Psalm 90:2 MSG)

From "once upon a time" to "kingdom come,"
God has always been our home. By his choice.

Then sad and beautiful dreams overtook [Eve],
which she would wake up from homesick
for a home she could no longer even name.

Frederick Buechner, *Beyond Words*

While Still a Long Way Off—Part 1

Story 1 was interrupted when Adam and Eve turned from God. That's when they lost their home.

Reclaiming what's been lost begins with returning to God. That's how we enter into Story 1.

But wait. You may be thinking, *I've never left God. Why do I need to return to him?* Great question. Leaving God can involve a tangible, physical moving away, but it can also be a subtle heart shift. We never stop believing. We never go anywhere. Yet our hearts grow numb.

Consider the story of the prodigal son—which, by the way, isn't what he's called in the story. It's how *we* have labeled him. God sees him in a different way. So does the father in the story. Speaking of the father, notice how the story starts and ends with him. He is the epicenter of it. And it's the story of two sons, not one.

> There was once a man who had two sons. The younger said to his father, "Father, I want right now what's coming to me."

A little like Adam and Eve wanted to become like gods "right now" by eating fruit from a tree that promised immediate results. Story 2 always appears to be a shortcut to greater freedom, power, and pleasure. At least initially. But when the money ran out and the son's circumstances declined, his view changed.

> That brought him to his senses. He said, "All those farmhands working for my father sit down to three meals a day, and here I am starving to death. I'm going back to my father. I'll say to him, Father, I've sinned against God, I've sinned before you; I don't deserve to be called your son. Take me on as a hired hand." He got right up and went home to his father.

The word *father* is used four times in four sentences. The son who initially wanted to get away from his father now can't quit thinking of his father ... and how he is his father's son.

> When he was still a long way off, his father saw him. His heart pounding, he ran out, embraced him, and kissed him.
>
> The son started his speech: "Father, I've sinned against God, I've sinned before you; I don't deserve to be called your son ever again." But the father wasn't listening. He was calling to the servants, "Quick. Bring a clean set of clothes and dress him. Put the family ring on his finger and sandals on his feet. Then get a prize-winning heifer and roast it. We're going to feast! We're going to have a wonderful time! My son is here—given up for dead and now alive! Given up for lost and now found!" And they began to have a wonderful time. (Luke 15:11–24 MSG)

The father wasn't listening to the son's Story 2 speech, because the father lived from Story 1 where a language of life, not blame, was spoken. He ran to hug his son, eager to close the gap between them.

And that concludes the story, right? Nope. That's just the story of the son who left and returned. Now let's look at the story of the other son. The one who stayed ... and also needed to return to his father.

While Still a Long Way Off—Part 2

With all the celebration over the return of the first son, it's easy to forget there was a second son. Many of us might see ourselves in him.

All this time his older son was out in the field. When the day's work was done he came in. As he approached the house, he heard the music and dancing. Calling over one of the houseboys, he asked what was going on. He told him, "Your brother came home. Your father has ordered a feast—barbecued beef!—because he has him home safe and sound."

Great news, right? The brother who stayed in his father's presence all this time must be overjoyed. Right? Actually, the opposite.

The older brother stomped off in an angry sulk and refused to join in. His father came out and tried to talk to him, but he wouldn't listen. The son said, "Look how many years I've stayed here serving you, never giving you one moment of grief, but have you ever thrown a party for me and my friends? Then this son of yours who has thrown away your money on whores shows up and you go all out with a feast!"

In the first half of the story, the father wouldn't listen to the younger son's Story 2 speech. Now it's the older son who won't listen to the Father's Story 1 speech. He can't grasp the concept of unconditional love after spending his life trying to earn his place at the table.

His father said, "Son, you don't understand. You're with me all the time, and everything that is mine is yours—but this is a wonderful time, and we had to celebrate. This brother of yours was dead, and he's alive! He was lost, and he's found!" (Luke 15:25–32 MSG)

The prize was never the father's inheritance. It was his presence. As it was in Eden.

You don't have to leave to come home. Nor do you have to feel lost to be found.

This is the heart of the Father. He walks with us in the cool of the garden and runs to us when we return. Yes, for those who appear to be a long way off. But also for those who are right at his side with their hearts far off.

Christopher Robin was putting on his Big Boots.
When he saw the Big Boots, Pooh knew
that an Adventure was going to happen,
and he brushed the honey off his nose with
the back of his paw, and spruced himself
up so as to look Ready for Anything.

A. A. Milne, *Christopher Robin Leads an Expedition*

The Hero's Journey

We're on a homeward journey. But the world is fascinated with a different kind of journey ... the Hero's Journey.

Joseph Campbell was a famous professor of literature who specialized in mythology. He had the gift of naming patterns that existed—including the beats of story that he observed in ancient mythology and modern times. He described this cycle in his 1949 book, *The Hero with a Thousand Faces*. The journey, or path, is represented by a circle where the hero travels into the unknown and must overcome great odds before returning back to the known world. We see this structure at play in what's come to be known as the Hero's Journey in almost every movie, from *The Wizard of Oz* to *Star Wars*.

The Hero's Journey is a human construct steeped in mythology that tries to make sense of the story we find ourselves in. It feels real because it mirrors the world we're born in. We don't expect our movie heroes to change all that much because, well, we don't tend to change all that much while in a Story 2 life. We do expect the protagonist to be different by the end of the movie. But different without God is just another version of Ecclesiastes. Even if you conclude the journey with more stuff, a new love, or a shiny prize, you still begin and end in Story 2. You start with you, leave with you, and end with you. Still an orphan longing for your true home.

If the Hero's Journey works without God, then it doesn't reflect the truest story. Without God, we may get a treasure . . . but never the pearl of great price. We may gain knowledge, but it comes from the Tree of Knowledge rather than the Tree of Life.

We're drawn to stories of epic good versus evil. It's essential to remember, however, that "good" alone isn't enough to save the day, the world, or us. Only God can do that. As C. S. Lewis stated, "There is but one good; that is God. Everything else is good when it looks to Him and bad when it turns from Him" (*The Great Divorce*).

In the end, the Hero's Journey is based on the wrong premise. It positions us as the hero and the answer to our story. It's storytelling where we get the outcome we want.

We don't play the major role. If we did, we'd probably go around bragging that we'd done the whole thing! No, we neither make nor save ourselves. God does both the making and saving. He creates each of us by Christ Jesus to join him in the work he does, the good work he has gotten ready for us to do, work we had better be doing. (Ephesians 2:10 MSG)

The Hero's Journey distorts reality by constructing stories where it's up to us to save the day or the world through our intelligence and strength. Yet we weren't made to succeed without God. We make ourselves the hero and then wonder why we don't see God do heroic things.

It's not possible for a person to succeed—I'm talking about eternal success—without heaven's help. (John 3:27 MSG)

The Hero's Journey can't provide that roadmap. But the Homeward Journey can. It offers the chance to regain what was lost in Eden.

Who We're Becoming

The Story 2 pull is toward quick answers and self-reliance—but God invites us into a far better story.

On the surface, Story 2 appears to offer more choices and fewer limitations. But Story 2 comes with a lot of disclaimers. It's a bit like the prescription commercials promising amazing health breakthrough with scenes of happy people—followed by the lengthy disclaimers stating all the ways we could die or suffer severe reactions from the very drug that is supposed to save us.

The problem with the self-made life is we are made for life with God at the center. Which is why the self-centered life never brings lasting fulfillment.

Story 2 is like a cosmic Whack-a-Mole game where the enemy tries to distract you from the fact that it never delivers. *That one didn't work for you? No worries. Try another. Whack away. There are millions to choose from. You can have any Story 2 story you want. Just keep moving and forget about Story 1. Why bring that one up anyway? Are you a Story 2 hater?*

The Homeward Journey is not about the shortest distance between two points. It's about the journey from who we are to who we're becoming. The goal isn't to get somewhere fast but to arrive a new creation.

In my all-time favorite novel, *The Paradise War*, author Stephen R. Lawhead powerfully describes this process through the thoughts of the main character, Lew.

> I could neither believe nor understand what had happened to me. For it seemed that something inside me had been awakened, some long-sleeping part of me had been roused to life. And now I could no longer be who I was before. But if I was no longer to be who I was, who was I to be?
>
> … How could I ever go back to the world I had known before? Truth to tell, I no longer considered going back a possibility. Here I was, by some miracle, and here I would stay.

Story 1 is a journey that, by design, awakens something inside us. Like Lew, once that long-sleeping part has been roused to life, we can't go back to the world we've known before. This new reality that we enter into pulsates with God's presence. We hunger for him. As my good friend Nancy says, "the deeper our dependence, the deeper God goes with us."

The ultimate triumph isn't some external elixir, title, or prize, but God. That's what the Eden Option is…returning to God with our whole heart.

> Then I will give them a heart to know Me, that I am the LORD; and they shall be My people, and I will be their God, for they shall return to Me with their whole heart. (Jeremiah 24:7 NKJV)

And it gets even better, because when we return, so does God.

> Return to me, and I will return to you, says the LORD of Heaven's Armies. (Zechariah 1:3 NLT)

That's the far better story. The one of who we're becoming along the way in our journey home.

It's what we trust in but don't yet see that keeps us going.
Do you suppose a few ruts in the road or rocks
in the path are going to stop us?
When the time comes, we'll be plenty ready
to exchange exile for homecoming.

2 Corinthians 5:7-8 MSG

St. Patrick's Hunger

St. Patrick, originally known as Patricius, was born around the year 400 in Rome. At sixteen he was kidnapped from his home in Britain by Irish slave traders. He spent six long years in isolation doing forced labor as a shepherd.

Scholar Thomas Cahill describes his season of captivity in his book *How the Irish Saved Civilization*:

> Patricius endured six years of this woeful isolation, and by the end of it he had grown from a careless boy to something he would surely never otherwise have become—a holy man, indeed a visionary for whom there was no longer any rigid separation between this world and the next. On his last night as Miliucc's slave, he received in sleep his first otherworld experience. A mysterious voice said to him: "Your hungers are rewarded: You are going home."

Don't we long for someone to tell us these same words? At last, our hunger is being rewarded. We're going to our true home. Don't we wish we were a visionary so in union with God that there's no longer any separation for us between this world and the next?

Though this world may empty us, only God can fill us. Our hungers remind us of our true home.

Jesus was clear that in this world we will have trouble. None of us get a pass on hard times. It's possible your hardest years might actually occur *after* you step into Story 1. Yet in a deeper way, they may be your best years since they are part of your journey with God.

That was the case for Patrick. After being kidnapped, he discovered life with God through years of isolation. But after entering into Story 1, he spent the next forty years living in poverty as he traveled the rugged terrain to bring light to a dark world. Later in his life, St. Patrick composed a prayer that has transcended the centuries. It focuses on God's protection as Creator and Father. Here's a portion of St. Patrick's Breastplate, forged through the fires of difficulty:

Christ with me, Christ before me, Christ behind me, Christ in me, Christ beneath me, Christ above me, Christ on my right, Christ on my left, Christ when I lie down, Christ when I sit down.

. . . I arise today through a mighty strength, the invocation of the Trinity, through belief in the Threeness, through confession of the Oneness of the Creator of creation.

Then there was Saul. As the top persecutor of Jewish believers in Jesus, he wielded his immense power with absolute conviction. But he did so under the false beliefs of a wrong story. After a miraculous transformation, God changed his name from Saul to Paul and he went on to write more New Testament books than anyone else. But would Paul's new life be easier in Story 1? Actually, just the opposite. God puts it this way:

I have handpicked him as my personal representative to non-Jews and kings and Jews. And now I'm about to show him what he's in for—the hard suffering that goes with this job. (Acts 9:15–16 MSG)

Story 1 doesn't guarantee an easy life. Just a meaningful one that echoes in eternity. As St. Patrick and Paul found out, it's the only story where our hungers for home are rewarded.

Trail or Trial?

As you're on this homeward journey, it's helpful to view it as being on a trail with God.

> The LORD says, "I will guide you along the best pathway for your life. I will advise you and watch over you." (Psalm 32:8 NLT)

God will be your guide, advising and watching over you. But there will also be obstacles. The enemy hates any move to greater intimacy with God. So he will oppose it. When he does, we have to be careful not to place God on trial, even subconsciously.

The words *trail* and *trial* are identical in spelling other than the "i" and "a" being reversed. But there's a world of difference between their meanings. One leads to intimacy. One leads to bitterness.

It's worth considering which word we take with us on our journey. One places us on a trail with God while the other places God on trial with us.

In Story 2, we are distant from God. Doubt about his goodness hangs in the air. In Story 1, we willingly and expectantly let him lead.

Do you see God as holding out on you ... or making a path for you? He desires for this to be a shared journey. One where he goes with us, before us, and beyond us.

But when we constantly evaluate God based on how we feel about our life, we open the door of doubt. What flows from doubt about God is never good. Remember, the only guarantee of Story 1 is God's presence. If we're in it for anything else, whatever it is can quickly become an idol. It becomes "the" thing or person or job that everything hinges on. If that happens, we lose our way. It's only a matter of time.

Be aware of this trap as you make this journey. God isn't on trial. But he is right there with you on the trail, guiding you homeward.

The enemy says you can't return home.
That's a lie.
He's the one who can't return home.
But we can.

The New Eden

I wish I could point to Eden on a map, physically travel to it, and politely ask the cherubim guarding the gates to lower their flaming swords and let me into paradise. But that's not how God designed it to work.

Instead, he promises us a New Eden. With him at the center of it all. Everything that's been lost will be made new. Including Eden. We will live there. In peace. Experiencing new adventures. Eating from the right tree.

Here's how John described it:

> Then the Angel showed me Water-of-Life River, crystal bright. It flowed from the Throne of God and the Lamb, right down the middle of the street. The Tree of Life was planted on each side of the River, producing twelve kinds of fruit, a ripe fruit each month. The leaves of the Tree are for healing the nations. Never again will anything be cursed. The Throne of God and of the Lamb is at the center.

His servants will offer God service—worshiping, they'll look on his face, their foreheads mirroring God. Never again will there be any night. No one will need lamplight or sunlight. The shining of God, the Master, is all the light anyone needs. And they will rule with him age after age after age. (Revelation 22:1–5 MSG)

This describes something real. Eden—not as it was, but Eden made new, for those who love God and anticipate walking with him in the cool of the garden. The author of Hebrews described it as a City built by God—encouraging us, like Abraham, to keep our eyes "on an unseen city with real, eternal foundations—the City designed and built by God" (Hebrews 11:10 MSG).

What is the purpose of this unseen yet real city designed and built by God? To infuse us with hope. To keep us moving forward in a world where most believers are stuck in the muck of Story 2.

In Proverbs, we read:

Hope deferred makes the heart sick, but a dream fulfilled is a tree of life. (13:12 NLT)

I love how the psalmist describes the exponential nature of this hope.

> A single day in your courts is better than a thousand anywhere else! I would rather be a gatekeeper in the house of my God than live the good life in the homes of the wicked. (Psalm 84:10 NLT)

For now, we can reclaim the story we were created for. That's choosing a Story 1 life in a Story 2 world. We do so not by looking backwards. Nor by forgetting we were made for Eden. But setting our eyes on the unseen city with real, eternal foundations. The City designed and built by God.

Our future home. The New Eden.

Make It Practical

We know where we're headed. That's good … and not enough.

Though the original Eden no longer exists on a map, God hasn't given up on the dream of Eden. He's actually created a New Eden that will be our future home one day. And for now, it's a beacon to guide us forward.

What does that look like? Because if we don't make it practical, we won't stay in it. The best description I've found is in the book of Hebrews, chapter 11. Pay attention to how the author describes the journey and how our longing for home makes it possible.

> The fundamental fact of existence is that this trust in God, this faith, is the firm foundation under everything that makes life worth living. It's our handle on what we can't see. The act of faith is what distinguished our ancestors, set them above the crowd. By faith, we

see the world called into existence by God's word, what we see created by what we don't see. (Hebrews 11:1–3 MSG)

Notice how the writer immediately declares that God is the foundation of it all. I love how the words evoke creation and the time of Eden. We're then given a list of people who ran this race well—including Noah, Abraham, Sarah, Joseph, Moses, Rahab, Samson, David and more. I encourage you to read Hebrews 11 in its entirety. You'll notice Adam and Eve failed to make the list. That's because the hallmark of a Story 1 life is a relentless desire for intimacy with God. It's a life of faith in God. Not doubt about God.

But what kept the faithful going? That's the million-dollar question! Let's pick up in verse 13.

Each one of these people of faith died not yet having in hand what was promised, but still believing. How did they do it? They saw it way off in the distance, waved their greeting, and accepted the fact that they were transients in this world.

This is such a helpful insight. They accepted that even in a Story 1 life, not everything will happen *in* this life. Better chapters are coming. So, like the father in the prodigal son story, we keep our eyes on the horizon, watching for what's to come, but never settling for this world as our true home.

> People who live this way make it plain that they are looking for their true home. If they were homesick for the old country, they could have gone back any time they wanted. But they were after a far better country than that—*heaven* country. You can see why God is so proud of them, and has a City waiting for them. (Hebrews 11:13–16 MSG)

They were homesick...but not for a Story 2 home. Not even a fantastic Story 2 home. They could return to that Ecclesiastes life anytime they wanted. But why would they? They were anticipating the New Eden. No longer a garden but a City that God built and had waiting for them.

Focusing on the journey *with* God and what was ahead kept them in Story 1. It's the same for us.

**Beware of going back
to what you once were,
when God wants you to be something
that you have never been.**

Oswald Chambers, *My Utmost for His Highest*

What Can We Experience Now?

Who do you trust your story to? For many years, I had the fear that my story would never be really known or rightly told. But like so much else, it really comes down to just two choices. Trust it with the One who longs to redeem it or just hope for the best.

A Story 2 world can't tell our stories properly. The world didn't get to define Jesus. Nor does it get to define us. But it is where our story plays out.

> I have given them your commands. And the world hates them because they don't fit in with it, just as I don't. I'm not asking you to take them out of the world, but to keep them safe from Satan's power. They are not part of this world any more than I am. (John 17:14–16 TLB)

Dear friends, I warn you as "temporary residents and foreigners" to keep away from worldly desires that wage war against your very souls. (1 Peter 2:11 NLT)

As we're on the Homeward Journey, it's important to remember our objective so we understand what can happen now … and what is to come.

Eden holds the answers to how Story 1 was lost and why we were born into a Story 2 world. But the goal isn't to return to the Eden of the past. That isn't God's invitation. He has created a new home for us, the city described in Hebrews. That is the New Eden. And we need to keep our eyes focused on it as we travel homeward.

But our journey isn't only focused on the promise of what is to come. The people in the Hebrews chapter were named because they were actively building and doing and risking things through faith.

Though we won't step into this New Eden until Jesus returns, God invites us to do things with him now that change the atmosphere for good. As we place God at the center of every aspect of our lives, we begin to regain and reclaim what we lost in Eden and what we were created for—life to the full (John 10:10).

There are four Eden attributes available to us right now:

- Eden Union: Reconnecting to the Vine
- Eden Voice: Restoring Our Original Roar
- Eden Vision: Re-Seeing Reality with a Reawakened Imagination
- Eden Rest: Receiving Real Restoration

Each Story 1 life will be as unique as the person living it. Stepping into it doesn't make us more like everyone else, but more fully who God made us to be. It's not a map of specific things to do but a way to see things differently.

We don't have to return to a tropical paradise like Eden for our lives to have these Eden qualities. We need to return to God being the center of our lives again. Everything flows from that.

I think you'll be blown away at how these four traits Adam and Eve gave away in Eden can be reclaimed in personal and practical ways as a regular part of your Story I life.

Eden Union:
Reconnect to the Vine

The Vine of Eden

We begin here because everything in Eden—and in Story 1—hinges on intimacy with God. The primary loss in Eden was union with God. It is what we most need to recover.

If Adam and Eve had loved God with their whole heart and mind, they would have never doubted his goodness or sought life apart from him. The Tree of Knowledge didn't take them closer to godhood but farther from God. It was a move from creation to chaos. And chaos, at its center, is empty and void.

Because of Adam and Eve's tragic choice, humanity became untethered from God. Into this void, God provides a lifeline. It is a living vine. And that vine is Jesus. He is the One by which everything, including Eden, was created. And, as God noted after the fall, it would be through him that everything would be made right once again.

Jesus is the vine that rescues us from the empty void of Story 2. Listen to his offer:

> Remain in me, as I also remain in you. No branch can bear fruit by itself; it must remain in the vine. Neither can you bear fruit unless you remain in me. I am the vine; you are the branches. If you remain in me and I in you, you will bear much fruit; apart from me you can do nothing. (John 15:4–5 NIV)

The invitation is to remain in him. Not come and go. Not seek him as a last resort. But to stay in active relationship with him. When we remain connected to the vine, we accomplish great things (bear much fruit). But when we disconnect, we remove ourselves from the source of life. Apart from Jesus, we can do nothing. Not do pretty well. Not pull it together in our own strength. Nothing.

Notice that as we can do nothing apart from Jesus, he does nothing on his own but stays in union with God in everything.

> I can do nothing on my own. I judge as God tells me. Therefore, my judgment is just, because I carry out the will of the one who sent me, not my own will. (John 5:30 NLT)

It is union with God that changes everything. Listen to the angel's message to Mary about the coming birth of Jesus:

> For with God nothing will be impossible. (Luke 1:37 NKJV)

The variable is whether we choose union with God by staying connected to Jesus. That's what takes us from Story 2 to Story 1. But believing in God isn't the same as staying in union with God. We become disconnected when we try to make life happen on our terms. In our timing. Through our strength. Doing so reflects the same foolish choice Adam and Eve made when they looked to the wrong tree for life.

> How foolish can you be? After starting your new lives in the Spirit, why are you now trying to become perfect by your own human effort? (Galatians 3:3 NLT)

Union with God or human effort. That was the choice in Eden and it is our choice now. Stay connected to the vine. Stay in Story 1.

Containers

C. S. Lewis wrote, "The soul is but a hollow which God fills" (*The Problem of Pain*).

If we don't allow God to fill our soul, something else will. Story 2 has endless options. But once we are filled with God's Spirit and connected to the vine, our lives are forever changed. That is Story 1.

Seeing everything as a container waiting to be filled will help you understand the world.

These various containers are only as true or good as what fills them. Like a bucket that can be emptied and re-filled with different substances, the meaning changes based on what's inside. A bucket labeled water is not safe to drink if filled with poison.

Though Story 2 tries to keep us focused on external appearances, Scripture reminds us that what's on the outside is never as important as what's on the inside.

> Now then, you Pharisees clean the outside of the cup and dish, but inside you are full of greed and wickedness. (Luke 11:39 NIV)

> For the LORD does not see as man sees; for man looks at the outward appearance, but the LORD looks at the heart. (1 Samuel 16:7 NKJV)

Our faith must rest with the Creator rather than in containers, which can and do change. We stumble when we assign permanent value or meaning to an earthly container. Containers change based on what they are filled with. Books and art and music aren't neutral. Or always good. Their goodness (or lack thereof) comes from what we fill them with.

Any creation untethered from the Creator will always be less than it could have been. Your favorite superhero, for instance, is an empty vessel waiting to be filled by the writer. A country's flag reflects the character of the country. As leadership changes, so does the meaning of the flag.

We are no different. It matters what we fill ourselves with. Especially when we're running on empty.

Jesus is the only One who can fill us with life.

> Jesus stood and shouted to the crowds, "Anyone who is thirsty may come to me! Anyone who believes in me may come and drink! For the Scriptures declare, 'Rivers of living water will flow from his heart.'" (John 7:37–39 NLT)

If we want to stay connected with God, it's essential that we allow him to fill us.

Eden Beacon
The Wise Men's North Star

From the moment of Adam and Eve's tragic choice in Eden, Jesus has been our only source for regaining Story 1.

We can't have a Story 1 life without an active, intimate relationship with Jesus.

Jesus *is* Story 1.

To enter it, we don't need a roadmap back to Eden. We simply need Jesus.

He is resolute to redeem what was lost in Eden. And there is nothing and no one in this world or the next that can prevent his mission.

God has put Christ over all rulers, authorities, powers, and kings, not only in this world but also in the next. (Ephesians 1:21 NCV)

It's fascinating how the magi, or "Wise Men," followed a star in their search for the birth of the prophesied King. In a literal sense, the star was guiding them to a stable in the middle of nowhere. But in a mythic sense, this "North Star" was guiding them back to "Eden"—not geographically, but to the One who would be the new Adam and make all things new.

And after they saw Jesus, they didn't go back to Herod with a report. Or go back to Story 2. They saw the miraculous, worshipped the baby Jesus, and followed him into Story 1.

We can too.

He's our North Star. He's how we experience Eden again. There is no other way.

God wants to be our perfect lover,
but instead we seek perfection in human relationships
and are disappointed when our lovers cannot love us
perfectly … We seek satisfaction of our spiritual longing
in a host of ways that may have very little to do with God.

Gerald May, *Addiction and Grace*

Intimacy Precedes Knowing

We are creative beings. With the Creator's DNA flowing through us, how could we not be?

Knowing our creativity is important. But knowing God is even more so.

Intimacy *with* God always precedes impact *for* God.

That's why we must begin here.

It is from this place of greater intimacy that greater insights, wisdom, and imagination begin to flow. Listen to this promise.

Call to me and I will answer you. I'll tell you marvelous and wondrous things that you could never figure out on your own.
(Jeremiah 33:3 MSG)

Here's how another translation puts it:

Ask me and I will tell you remarkable secrets you do not know about things to come. (NLT)

But notice the condition: We must call to God and ask him to tell us. In other words, it is through union with God that we discover greater insights far beyond our ability to know.

God infused you with gifts before you were born. He gave you specific passions so the two of you could pursue them together. The more you know God, the more you discover your true identity and purpose.

But "doing" isn't the most important thing to God. He created Adam and Eve and loved them fully before they did one thing.

It's freeing to realize not everything is up to you. As I say in my book *The Story of With*, "God doesn't need your help as much as he wants your heart. Whenever you start to focus more on your talents and gifts than on him, you miss the main invitation. Which is to pursue them together. With him."

He values intimacy over productivity. Relationship over accomplishments. What is done in your own strength ultimately comes to nothing. But what is done in union with God has the power to transcend you and ripple far beyond this moment in time.

The Heart of
the Matter

Before we move from the topic of union, we must address the heart.

Actually, God tells us to start with the heart.

> Guard your heart above all else, for it determines the course of your life. (Proverbs 4:23 NLT)

The heart matters immensely to God. Far more than our actions or words.

> These people . . . honor me with their lips, but their hearts are far from me. (Isaiah 29:13 NLT)

Jesus understood the importance of our hearts as well. He defined his mission by quoting from the scrolls of Isaiah (61:1) saying he came to heal the brokenhearted and set the captives free.

The enemy understands this too. He opposes your union with God more than anything else. That's why he tries to get you to doubt God's heart and neglect your heart.

To state the obvious, an awakened heart is essential to the Story 1 life.

It's essential we care for our hearts on a daily basis. There are many ways to do so. Read Scripture. Listen to soundtracks or classical music. Take a walk in nature. Bring your questions to God and journal the conversation. Make something beautiful. Be fully present. Choose love over fear.

The condition of our heart also affects our impact on people and projects. No significant relationship or work happens without an engaged heart. It's impossible to make another heart beat faster when ours has flatlined. Everything we do flows—or doesn't—from the heart.

A good man brings good things out of the good stored up in his heart, and an evil man brings evil things out of the evil stored up in

his heart. For the mouth speaks what the heart is full of.
(Luke 6:45 NIV)

Thankfully, God takes the lead in restoring our hearts. If we ask.

> Create in me a new, clean heart, O God, filled with clean thoughts and right desires. (Psalm 51:10 TLB)

> I will give you one heart and a new spirit; I will take from you your hearts of stone and give you tender hearts of love for God, so that you can obey my laws and be my people, and I will be your God. (Ezekiel 11:19–20 TLB)

Nothing will help you stay in Story 1 more than caring for your heart. Make it your top priority. For it determines the course of your life.

A faith that moves mountains is a faith that expands horizons. It does not bring us into a smaller world full of easy answers, but into a larger one where there is room for wonder.

Rich Mullins, Thoughts and Reflections from
The World as Best as I Remember It

Eden Voice:
Restore Your Roar

Trust GOD from the bottom of your heart;
don't try to figure out everything on your own.
Listen for GOD's voice in
everything you do,
everywhere you go;
he's the one who will keep you on track.
Don't assume that you know it all.
Run to GOD!
Run from evil!

Proverbs 3:5-7 MSG

Eden Voices

In our journey to regain what was lost in Eden, we now look at the role voices played in creation, paradise, and the fall.

It was through the literal loss of my voice that God introduced me to Story 1. The return of it was breathtaking. But learning how to use my voice to share Story 1 has been an even greater adventure.

As part of that journey, I've come to see how God's voice—and ours—has been under attack since the beginning.

God's voice was the spark and force of creation.

He created the heavens and the earth by speaking things into existence. He spoke light and land and sky and oceans and animals of every kind. But he didn't just speak Adam into being, he also breathed the breath of life into his body after forming it from the dust of the earth (Genesis 2:7).

After creating Adam and Eve, he spoke a blessing over them and then excitedly told them all he had created for them (Genesis 1:28–29). And he used his voice to invite them into the garden—as well as warn them of the one tree to avoid.

God also gave Adam and Eve their voices.

As their Father, he taught them how to speak. Adam used his voice and creativity to name the wild animals (Genesis 2:19–20) as well as to speak poetry and express awe upon seeing Eve for the first time (Genesis 2:23). Like his Father, Adam used his voice for good.

But then Adam and Eve listened to the wrong voice. The enemy's strategy was three-fold. He wanted them to doubt God's voice, listen to his voice, and silence their voice. It worked incredibly well for him in Eden, and he continues to use it against us today.

In the crucial moment when Eve offered Adam the fruit, he said nothing (Genesis 3:6). By not using his voice when it mattered most, he began to lose it.

After rejecting the Tree of Life, Adam's and Eve's voices no longer spoke life. Instead, they mimicked the language of the serpent and the Tree of Knowledge. It was void of love and filled with doubt and fear. Their first words after the fall are ones of shame and blame—justifying why they were hiding and blaming God, each other, and the serpent for eating from the wrong tree (Genesis 3:10–13).

After God banished them from Eden, they went silent. They didn't just lose Eden. They lost their voices. And along with it, their primary place in the story God was telling.

A Story 1 life requires the recovery of our Eden voice.

Why Jesus Spoke Stories

Jesus used his voice to speak life to everyone he encountered. But he didn't simply convey information. He told parables that revealed Story 1 concepts to those stuck in a Story 2 world.

Why did Jesus choose the format of story rather than just stating facts? His disciples asked him that question directly. And Jesus gave an equally direct response.

The disciples came up and asked, "Why do you tell stories?" [Jesus] replied, "You've been given insight into God's kingdom. You know how it works. Not everybody has this gift, this insight; it hasn't been given to them. Whenever someone has a ready heart for this, the insights and understandings flow freely. But if there is no readiness, any trace of receptivity soon disappears. That's why I tell stories: to create readiness, to nudge the people toward a welcome awakening. (Matthew 13:10–13 MSG)

Don't miss why Jesus said he told stories. First, to create readiness. Second, to nudge people toward a welcome awakening. In other words, Jesus used his voice to tell stories to help us find our story.

We've been given a voice to speak light into a dark world. To speak love over fear. Creation over chaos.

When we use our voice in this way, we begin to recover our Eden voice. When we speak words that have an eternal spark, I refer to that as our roar. Because it has a beauty and strength to it that transcends us.

How are you wielding your voice? Does it reverberate with strength? Create a readiness in those who hear it? Nudge people toward a welcome awakening?

That's why Jesus told stories. It's the language of Story 1.

Eden Beacon
Aslan's Song of Creation

In *The Magician's Nephew*, C. S. Lewis offers this imaginary, fantastical look at the world's creation through Aslan's voice:

In the darkness, something was happening at last. A voice had begun to sing. It was very far away and Digory found it hard to decide from which direction it was coming. Sometimes it seemed to come from all directions at once. Sometimes he almost thought it was coming out of the earth beneath them. Its lower notes were deep enough to be the voice of the earth herself. There were no words. There was hardly even a tune. But it was, beyond comparison, the most beautiful noise he had ever heard. It was so beautiful he could hardly bear it ....

Then two wonders happened at the same moment. One was that the voice was suddenly joined by other voices; more voices than you could possibly count. They were in harmony with it, but far higher up the scale: cold, tingling, silvery voices. The second wonder was that the blackness overhead, all at once, was blazing with stars. They didn't come out gently one by one, as they do on a summer evening. One moment there had been nothing but darkness; next moment a thousand, thousand points of light leaped out—single stars, constellations, and planets, brighter and bigger than any in our world.

In this fictionalized account, darkness is penetrated by a voice. A singing voice. The voice of the great lion, Aslan. Then his voice is joined by other voices. And from that song, creation begins. With a creative roar.

Things Hidden Since the World's First Day

Have you considered Jesus as an Eden storyteller?

On a macro level, all things were created in and through Jesus. Including the creation of Eden and the idea of story (John 1:1–5). But it didn't stop there. While telling stories, Jesus shared this jaw-dropping insight with his followers. Jesus revealed that his stories serve as beacons to Eden by bringing into the open things hidden since the world's first day.

> All Jesus did that day was tell stories—a long storytelling afternoon. His storytelling fulfilled the prophecy: I will open my mouth and tell stories; I will bring out into the open things hidden since the world's first day. (Matthew 13:34–35 MSG)

I love the wordplay here. Jesus *opened* his mouth to bring things out into the *open*. As sons and daughters of the Creator, we're invited to do the same. But notice how the enemy tried to derail this. After Adam and Eve chose the Tree of Knowledge, they hid from God. Rather than bringing things out into the open that had been hidden, they became the hidden. As Adam puts it,

> I was afraid because I was naked, so I hid. (Genesis 3:10 NIV)

We hide from God as well, mostly from shame, doubt, and fear. As long as we remain hidden within Story 2, we can't use our voice to bring into the open things hidden since the world's first day.

When we step into Story 1, we regain our voice and are invited to participate in revealing what was hidden. The world could use the help. Perhaps because Story 2 has its roots in the Tree of Knowledge, people who live in that story are convinced self-knowledge is the key to all the answers.

God wants to reveal things to us in a radical Story 1 way. Look at how the psalmist Asaph, the prophet Isaiah, and the apostle Paul describe the mystery.

My people, hear my teaching; listen to the words of my mouth. I will open my mouth with a parable; I will utter hidden things, things from of old—things we have heard and known, things our ancestors have told us. We will not hide them from their descendants; we will tell the next generation the praiseworthy deeds of the LORD, his power, and the wonders he has done. (Psalm 78:1–4 NIV)

From now on I will tell you of new things, of hidden things unknown to you. They are created now, and not long ago; you have not heard of them before today. So you cannot say, "Yes, I knew of them." (Isaiah 48:6–7 NIV)

Our words are wise because they are from God, telling of God's wise plan to bring us into the glories of heaven. This plan was hidden in former times, though it was made for our benefit before the world began. But the great men of the world have not understood it; if they had, they never would have crucified the Lord of Glory. (1 Corinthians 2:7–8 TLB)

What's been hidden since the time of Eden is meant to be found. And we get to participate in the process . . . through our creative roar.

Discovering Your Voice

What exactly is your voice?

It's not simply the vibrational sound that comes out when you talk. We're after something far deeper than that.

Your voice is the way, with God, you can change the atmosphere for good through your presence and talents. Your Eden voice won't sound like anyone else because no one else has lived your story. It is shaped and influenced by a unique convergence of things such as ...

Your early childhood experiences.   How you experienced play.

The scars of your story.

What you're drawn to.   How you process information.

The effect you have on a room when you enter it. And leave it.

Your curiosity, wonder, and awe for God.

How easily you laugh at life ... and yourself.

How well you love others.   How freely you cry.

If your heart is alive or shut down.

Whether your decisions are driven by fear or love.

Who or what you look to for validation.

If your identity is tied more to what you do... or who you are.

Now imagine tossing all of these ingredients into a cosmic blender. This one-of-a-kind concoction is your signature drink. Your one-of-a-kind voice. No one else has it. Or can duplicate it.

Don't keep this elixir bottled up. Don't water it down. Keep it full-strength. And drink it daily.

Bottoms up!

Until the lion learns to write,
every story will always
glorify the hunter.

African Proverb

Your Creative Roar

Now that you understand your unique Eden voice, it's important for you to use it. Otherwise, you'll begin to lose it.

As we saw earlier, Adam remained silent as the serpent tempted Eve. From that point forward, his voice grew weaker. In Story 2, it went completely silent.

But the more you use your voice, the more powerful it becomes. Your creative roar represents the full power of your unique voice … once you learn the purpose and the power of it.

In the first chapter of Genesis, we see the power of God speaking things into existence.

When you speak, you are doing the same thing. You are bringing something new into existence through your presence and your gifting.

The problem is that the world tries to convince us that the only way for us to be heard is by sounding like whoever is popular at the moment. That's a mistake. We diminish our voice when we try to sound like others. Because no one wants an echo of what they've already heard.

Even if you don't know what to do with it yet, the voice God gave you is completely unique ... by design.

So don't try to be like _____ (fill in the blank). We already have that person's flavor, color, voice, look. It was original when it was first spoken, not when it's repeated. The more our voice sounds like others, the more it blends in with the noise of the world. Story 2 trains us to be passive consumers and critiquers of what is. Story 1 invites us to join God as creators of what could be.

God made you utterly unique. Embrace that. Speak what only you can bring to life. If you don't, you'll miss what you were born to do. As will everyone your voice was meant to awaken.

Stop doing what's been overdone so you can start doing what's never been done ... as only you can. Let your art blaze with God's trueness and your unique signature. Then invite us there. Through your creative roar.

The desert beckons us, as the long winding road did for Bilbo Baggins or the mystery of the wardrobe for Lucy Pevensie. What would Narnia be without this little girl choosing to press forward into the snowy evergreens toward the lamppost?
She could have turned her back and shut the door, but we're thankful she didn't.
Without her response, we would not know Aslan.

Cara L. T. Murphy, *The Inquisitive Christ*

Now Is the Time

If you're wondering when to use the voice God has given you, consider this: He could have designated your time on earth to be decades or even centuries ago … but he chose now. For such a time as this.

When you create with the Creator, you bring beauty, life, and order into this chaotic world. Your gifting isn't meant to sit on the sidelines, waiting until things are less chaotic. God-given creativity is meant to counter the chaos, changing the atmosphere for good.

All of creation longs for the return of the true story that was lost in Eden. It's waiting for the return of Jesus when all things will be made new. But perhaps it is also eagerly awaiting the sons and daughters of God to discover and use our voices too.

> For we know that all creation has been groaning as in the pains of childbirth right up to the present time. (Romans 8:22 NLT)

But if we choose to remain silent, God will accomplish his purposes by other means.

> For if you remain completely silent at this time, relief and deliverance will arise for the Jews from another place, but you and your father's house will perish. Yet who knows whether you have come to the kingdom for such a time as this? (Esther 4:14 NKJV)

Some words hold more power than others. The Greek term *logos* represents a more general use of language or words. *Rhema*, on the other hand, refers to the living, spoken word. It is a more particular word that has greater significance.

We see a similar distinction with the concept of time. The Greek word *chronos* refers to time in general. It's where we get the word *chronological*. It represents the ordinary movement of time. The word *kairos* has a more specific meaning. It refers to "now" time, as in "For such a *kairos* as this" (Esther 4:14).

As we recover our voice in Story 1, we have the ability to speak specific *rhema* words for this specific *kairos* time.

And the enemy hates that. As in Eden, he will try to silence our voice. Especially for such a time as this. He says no. But God says now.

We're not promised tomorrow. He has given you your voice for such a time as this.

> Then I heard the voice of the Lord saying, "Whom shall I send? And who will go for us?" And I said, "Here am I. Send me!" (Isaiah 6:8 NIV)

We were created for this moment to speak, love, and create in this moment. Now is the time.

But it doesn't stop there. Now that we've found our Eden voice, it's time to enhance our vision.

The eyes of the LORD search the whole earth in order to strengthen those whose hearts are fully committed to him.

2 Chronicles 16:9 NLT

Eden Vision:
Re-See Reality

Keeping your eyes on Jesus
is the best way
to keep your eyes on Eden.

Seeing What's Real

On our Homeward Journey, the power of sight is essential. In Eden, so much was lost because of how Adam and Eve chose to see God ... and themselves. That we why we must reclaim our vision.

How we see the world is so essential. When God is at the center, our vision is focused. But the farther we get from him, the less we see what's real. Our vision becomes blurred.

Perhaps because we have a tree in our eye.

> And why worry about a speck in your friend's eye when you have a log in your own? How can you think of saying to your friend, "Let me help you get rid of that speck in your eye," when you can't see past the log in your own eye? Hypocrite! First get rid of the log in your own eye; then you will see well enough to deal with the speck in your friend's eye. (Matthew 7:3–5 NLT)

Have you noticed so much comes back to trees? In the garden. In our lives. In our eyes. Adam and Eve chose the wrong tree. Then they hid from God among the bushes. The Tree of Knowledge is the biggest log of all. It affects how we see everything. Including the story we live in. As we traded God's reality for that of our own making, we didn't just lose true knowledge. We lost our sight.

> They do not know, nor do they understand, for He has smeared over their eyes so that they cannot see, and their hearts so that they cannot comprehend. (Isaiah 44:18 NASB)

Blind spots affect how we see life, God, ourselves, others … and our story.

Thankfully, Jesus came to help us regain our sight. A simple yet powerful prayer is "Jesus, show me how you see things. Let me see what's really going on. Open my eyes to your deeper reality."

Remember the story where Jesus touched the blind man twice? After the first time, the man said the people looked like trees. Once again. Trees.

> The man looked around. "Yes," he said, "I see people, but I can't see them very clearly. They look like trees walking around."

So Jesus touched him a second time. And then, well, here's how Scripture puts it:

> Then Jesus placed his hands on the man's eyes again, and his eyes were opened. His sight was completely restored, and he could see everything clearly. (Mark 8:24–25 NLT)

That's what we're after here. To see things clearly. To see the decisions each day through the lens of Story 1 and Story 2 options. For that to happen, we need to take our eyes off the trees, off the enemy, off ourselves, and off our screens. We need to be more present by turning our eyes to Jesus.

What we're after is his vision of us and for us.

I will pour out my Spirit on all people.
Your sons and daughters will prophesy,
your young men will see visions,
your old men will dream dreams.

Acts 2:17 NIV

Lack of Vision

When I am stuck, it's almost always due to a vision problem. More accurately, a lack of vision.

The solution is often right in front of me if I would just open my eyes … and my hands. My refusal to do so reminds me of the story I heard of some shortsighted monkeys.

Hunters in Africa had a problem with wild monkeys creating mayhem in their village. So they developed an ingenious yet simple way to capture these clever animals. They placed a peanut within heavy jars at the base of trees in the nearby jungle. They then tied one end of the rope around the base of each container and hid several feet away in the foliage. With the other end of the rope in their hands, the trap was set.

An unsuspecting monkey would come across a bottle, sniff out the snack, and thrust his paw inside. The opening was just wide enough for the paw to fit in—but not for his peanut-holding fist to come out. The monkey now had a dilemma. The jar was too heavy to move, yet there was no way to get the peanut out. The fixation on the prize kept the monkey stuck. All he had to do was release his grip and run to freedom. But the monkey refused to let go even as the hunter slowly pulled the rope—and him—to captivity.

I'm that monkey more often than I care to admit. Perhaps you can relate. Our ironclad grip keeps all of us stuck by keeping our focus on the wrong things. But remember, the problem is a vision problem. When we open our eyes to what God is up to, our grip loosens and our options increase.

> If people can't see what God is doing, they stumble all over themselves; but when they attend to what he reveals, they are most blessed. (Proverbs 29:18 MSG)

When I catch myself saying things like "The way it looks to me" and "The way I see it," that's a dead giveaway I have a vision problem.

Refocusing my vision by asking God for his interpretation rather than mine is always the first step to restoring my Eden vision.

I can see, and that is why I can be happy, in what
you call the dark, but which to me is golden.
I can see a God-made world, not a manmade world.

Helen Keller

Eden Beacon

Fruits of Creation

There were two trees in the center of the garden, each producing a different kind of fruit. The fruits led to a choice that continues to ripple through our world.

In the New Testament, we learn of nine fruits. These aren't produced by a tree but by the Spirit.

> The Holy Spirit produces this kind of fruit in our lives: love, joy, peace, patience, kindness, goodness, faithfulness, gentleness, and self-control. (Galatians 5:22 NLT)

It's safe to assume the Spirit always had these fruits. So what role did those fruits play in creation and in Eden? Could it be that Adam and Eve had access to these fruits in Eden? Or that they were present in the Tree of Life?

Either way, the nine fruits would have been a powerful antidote to the appeal of the Tree of Knowledge of Good and Evil.

Love would have countered the fear that God was holding out.

Joy would have kept their desires focused on the right tree.

Peace would have eroded the restlessness that caused them to strive for a self-driven life.

Patience would have countered the impatience of taking matters into their own hands.

Kindness and gentleness would have helped them not blame everyone but themselves for their choice.

Goodness would have been gained without a tree that offered good only with evil.

Faithfulness would have taken away the doubt of God's character.

As for self-control, well, with that in place, Eden would never have been lost.

If only Adam and Eve had embraced the fruits of the Spirit in Eden.

**Taste and see
that the LORD is good.**

Psalm 34:8 NIV

Respect Your Story

One of the most essential things is seeing yourself as God does.

In Eden, Adam and Eve were fully seen, known, and loved. When we look to God for our identity, we begin to see what's possible in terms of not just who we are ... but what we do.

As you step more fully into Story 1, it's good to be curious about how God might upgrade your talents and interests.

Consider the fishermen before they met Jesus in Galilee. They excelled at their craft. Fishing likely brought these men some level of joy, but then Jesus invited them into something truer. In an instant, expert fishermen became "fishers of men." They traded the foreshadowing of their prior calling for a full measure of what they were born to be.

A friend of mine is an eye surgeon. She restores sight. That's her profession and she's good at it. But one day she realized if money wasn't an issue, she'd rather write stories. That felt like such a disconnect from the trajectory of her career. I pointed out that there was actually a clear link between the two. Her passion was to help people see. That was her true calling. But her deeper love was writing stories. Rather than a detour from what she'd been doing, God was inviting her to help people see in an entirely new way—through story.

When you think back on your life, what have you always been drawn to? I'm not asking what others say you do well. You can be good at doing things that you have little interest in. I'm talking about activities that cause you to lose track of time when you enter into them. What would it look like to experience that joy again, in a fresh new way?

I don't recommend you quit your current job in the hopes that someone will immediately begin paying you for what you most love to do. That would be nice … but it rarely happens that way.

A kinder first step is to remember what used to bring you joy. Don't minimize this as a waste of time or pointless. Respect the process. The original meaning of the word *re-spect* actually meant to "re-see." That's what we're after here. To re-see what we've long quit looking for.

The more time we spend in Story 1, the more God strengthens us. What was lost, forgotten, or previously unseen can be restored. Not just to the level it was before, but better than before.

As you enter into this discovery process, stay with God and stay expectant. Hints of your Story 1 life may be right before your eyes, like they were for the eye surgeon and fishermen.

Red Sea Moments

As long as a situation looks impossible, we're not seeing it as God does.

Our limited view suggests we have only a few options, none of them good. Yet God has endless options.

In those situations, first ask the God of infinite possibilities for a vision upgrade. Then, keep your eyes on Jesus rather than on the situation at hand.

> Keep your eyes on Jesus, our leader and instructor.
> (Hebrews 12:2 TLB)

Moses discovered this with Pharaoh's army closing in on one side and the Red Sea on the other side. The situation looked hopeless, until he traded the Israelites' lack of vision for a new vision that included God.

Moses told the people, "Don't be afraid. Just stand still and watch the LORD rescue you today. The Egyptians you see today will never be seen again. The LORD himself will fight for you. Just stay calm." (Exodus 14:14 NLT)

I love how Moses addressed the issue of vision here. Look, he told the people. Yes, you see the problem before you. But the problem you see today will never be seen again.

We've been talking a lot about the power in seeing things more clearly. But some things we never need to see again.

When we see God more clearly than our problems, we no longer fear. We can stay calm in our Red Sea moments because we know God will fight for us. He is our rescuer.

That's a powerful vision upgrade.

**You can't depend on your eyes
when your imagination is out of focus.**

Mark Twain,
A Connecticut Yankee in King Arthur's Court

The Risk of Imagination

We think the fall occurred when Adam and Eve ate from the wrong tree. But in a sense, Eden was lost the moment they listened to the serpent. Because in that moment, they imagined God holding out on them—and what life could be if they took matters into their own hands.

God had seen the way imagination had been misused before Eden. Lucifer was one of the most powerful angelic beings. At some point, he imagined overtaking God and being the center of the story. So he told that story to other angels, asking them to imagine that future. And one third of these created beings brazenly put their trust in another created being, Lucifer, over their Creator. Soon after, the war in heaven became a reality ... and the rebellious angels were defeated and kicked out of God's kingdom.

After that, no one would have blamed God if he didn't infuse Adam and Eve with an imagination. Because the risk was they could use it to imagine life without him. But in his generosity and good heart, God chose to continue to bestow imagination on humanity.

Tragically, the serpent wooed them to doubt God's goodness and imagine how it would be if they were like God. Eve ate from the wrong tree. And then Adam, who couldn't imagine life without her, ate the forbidden fruit as well. When we leave God out of our imagination, things go south really fast.

> The LORD observed the extent of human wickedness on the earth, and he saw that everything they thought or imagined was consistently and totally evil. (Genesis 6:5 NLT)

And later, the psalmist makes a similar chilling observation:

> From their callous hearts comes iniquity; their evil imaginations have no limits. (Psalm 73:7 NIV)

Yet God entrusted the immense power of an imagination to you and me. He took great risk in giving us this gift. Yet many, if not most, will use it to imagine a future without God. Story 2 is populated with people doing just that.

That's why it's so important for those of us in Story 1 to submit our imagination to God and use it for good. To combine a God-healed memory of our past with a God-fueled imagination of the future.

What stands against that, as always, is the enemy's attempt to fuse our imagination from God with doubt about God. He's seen it work so many times before. But we don't have to fall for it. Instead, we can stand against the enemy's attacks, knowing he will flee (James 4:7).

Story 2 tries to make God not just irrelevant . . . but boring. A practical way to protect our imagination is to remain more fascinated with the Creator than our creations. In his novel *Les Misérables*, Victor Hugo describes a bishop this way: "He wasn't a man who studied God but was dazzled by God." Yes, that's it.

Imagination is an incredibly powerful weapon, but in the right hands it offers far more than an escape from reality. It can be used to penetrate the fog of Story 2 to show God's deeper reality.

He wasn't a man who studied God
but was dazzled by God.

Victor Hugo, *Les Misérables*

Create with the Creator

When we reclaim our Eden imagination, God can use it in ways we never imagined.

God invites us into the new by putting us in the middle of what we never imagined doing, only for us to discover we can't imagine doing anything else. But to experience it, we have to be willing to enter into the unknown with God.

It's a journey that doesn't just provide a change in scenery but creates a change in us. We begin seeing life one way—but by the last mile, we're no longer the same. We don't just arrive somewhere new. We become new along the way. In ways we couldn't imagine that actually expand our imagination.

God doesn't just initiate these journeys. He goes with us and works within us.

God can do anything, you know—far more than you could ever imagine or guess or request in your wildest dreams! He does it not by pushing us around but by working within us, his Spirit deeply and gently within us. (Ephesians 3:20–21 MSG)

The best ideas rarely come on demand. Nor do we tend to see them when we're impatient or distracted. Poet Ruth Stone, while working the fields, would have poems come at her. "It was like a thunderous train of air and it would come barreling down at her over the landscape." If she didn't capture it, the words would "continue on across the landscape looking for another poet."*

Ideas tend to show up in the least expected moments. Right before we fall asleep, in the silence of a drive or walk, during a long hot shower, or on the deck as we watch the sun rise or set. When we have time to breathe. We often miss them because they initially don't seem like something important. The ideas are never fully formed. If they were, why would they need us?

. . . .

*From Elizabeth Gilbert's talk, *Your Elusive Creative Genius.*

Unlike instant coffee, the best ideas need time to percolate. They intrigue and woo us but refuse to give away their secrets too easily. They'll keep us up at night, then disappear as we wake. They invite us to chase them but also to savor them. This explains the feelings of restless discontent you sometimes have. It's totally normal. Because you've caught a glimpse of something before it has form. You see what others can't. Not what is but what could be.

Rather than dismiss something the world has no name for yet, give it time to develop. The first of anything rarely comes out fully formed ... or with any guarantees. So don't get tripped up when an idea won't let you go and others don't understand you. That's okay. The Creator does. He thought of the idea before you did. And he thought enough of you to trust you with it.

See your imagination as an invitation to create with the Creator once again. As it was in Eden.

Eden Rest:

Real Restoration

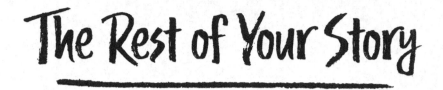

The Rest of Your Story

We now come to the fourth attribute lost in Eden. One that has plagued every human since the loss of paradise.

The ability to rest. Not work until we're exhausted just to crash, re-charge, and wake to do it again.

Real, restorative rest. It isn't part of the Story 2 Ecclesiastes life. But we get it back in Story 1.

Perhaps the best place to start is with God. On the seventh day of creation, we're told that God rested.

> Then God blessed the seventh day and made it holy, because on it he rested from all the work of creating that he had done.
> (Genesis 2:3 NIV)

But what does that mean? God wasn't exhausted. He didn't work up a sweat. He could have created every day for millions of years and never repeated himself. Every day another new creation.

> As we enter into God's faith-rest life we cease from our own works, just as God celebrates his finished works and rests in them.
> (Hebrews 4:10 TPT)

Mark Twain is said to have made this wry observation about creation: "Man was made at the end of the week's work, when God was tired." That says more about humanity than God. It's funny, but the part about God isn't accurate. Isaiah reminds us,

> Do you not know? Have you not heard? The Lord is the everlasting God, the Creator of the ends of the earth. He will not grow tired or weary, and his understanding no one can fathom. He gives strength to the weary and increases the power of the weak.
> (Isaiah 40:28–29 NIV)

God doesn't grow weary. He wasn't tired. He had the same full strength after the days of creation that he had before he began. And he has endless reserves of strength and power to give to anyone who needs it.

But he did treat the seventh day uniquely.

I believe God was taking time to savor and celebrate his creativity and to model for us what our rhythm of work, worship, and restoration should look like. I find it fascinating that Adam's first full day of life was the seventh day. The day of rest.

On this day, God stopped doing more, at least momentarily, to experience what he'd done. He took in all that he had made. He fully saw it. He enjoyed it. He blessed it. He made it holy. He paused from creating. And he proclaimed it good as he savored his creation...perhaps with Adam.

Let's follow his example by taking time to pause and savor what we have created with the Creator. When we see it as God does, we can proclaim it good rather than just call it done.

Hurry Is an Attitude

Years ago I was with a friend, expressing how busy my life had become. John Moorhead was a generation older and had accomplished many great things in his life. But he was never in a hurry.

I, on the other hand, was always in a hurry. Multitasking was my response to a world that wouldn't slow down. I began each morning at full speed, measured the day's success by how productive and efficient I was, collapsed each night in bed, and hit repeat. I wasn't looking for a solution because I didn't believe I had a problem. I just wanted him to know the reality of all I was juggling. Yes, it's a lot. But I'm doing it.

He waited patiently until I ran out of words. Then, after a minute of silence, he met my eyes with empathy.

"Allen, have you ever considered that hurry is an attitude?"

I looked at him as if he'd said the earth was flat.

He smiled. "I'm serious. Hurry is an attitude that comes from an agreement with a lie."

I leaned in. "What's the lie?"

"That God expects more of us than we can do each day. Hurry isn't inevitable. It's just an attitude."

Tears filled my eyes. And something rose within me that I hadn't felt in a long time: hope that when the sun rose tomorrow, I could be a new, unhurried man.

John is in the kingdom now, but his words have colored every aspect of my life, including my creativity. It's impossible to breathe life into others or my art when I'm running so fast I can't catch my own breath.

Jesus understands—and offers a far better alternative.

> Are you tired? Worn out? Burned out on religion? Come to me. Get
> away with me and you'll recover your life. I'll show you how to take a

real rest. Walk with me and work with me—watch how I do it. Learn the unforced rhythms of grace. I won't lay anything heavy or ill-fitting on you. Keep company with me and you'll learn to live freely and lightly. (Matthew 11:28–30 MSG)

Let him replace your hurry with his unforced rhythms of grace. Eden rest is available in Story 1.

Don't copy the behavior and customs of this world,
but be a new and different person
with a fresh newness in all you do and think.
Then you will learn from your own experience
how his ways will really satisfy you.

Romans 12:2 TLB

Stuck in Permanent Survival Mode

In busy times, it's easy to get stuck in permanent survival mode.

It's not hard to see why. The world's treadmill has sped up and is only getting faster. And so we speed up as well. Do more in less time, and with no time to fill our tank with things that restore us or provide rest. Over time, we seek relief over restoration. Dreams fall by the wayside. It's okay, we think. We'll get back to it when things are less busy. Yet that time rarely comes.

Over time, the less time we spend on what makes us come alive . . . makes us feel less alive. Less true to who we were created to be.

Though it might not seem true in your weariness, who God created you to be matters immensely. Your ability to change the world for good matters far more than you imagine ... when you pursue it with God.

So remember, no matter how chaotic this moment is, you were born for such a time as this (Esther 4:14). To make a difference in such a time as this. But it's essential to go at the pace your soul was created for.

When nothing seems to be coming together, here are three simple ways to get unstuck:

1) Live more before trying to make more happen.

2) Reject the lie that you have to be an expert. No one ever feels 100 percent qualified or ready.

3) Stop approaching the situation as if it's all up to you when God offers his presence.

God is really good at setting us free.

> *It is for freedom* that Christ has set us free. (Galatians 5:1 NIV)

He's ready to do so right now ... if we'll invite him into our stuck places.

In the eye of the storm, choose restoration.

In the madness of the moment, choose to be present to those who matter most.

In the chaos, choose calm.

Doing so provides Eden rest.

Under Construction

My high school senior and I were having a hard night at home. I'd gotten us tickets to a movie for a father-son night together. But things were quickly derailing.

He had a few chores to do before we left but was stalling and complaining. I could feel my heart tanking.

By the time the chores were finally done, so was I. Everything in me wanted to call off the plans.

Yet I sensed God's nudge to not lose this time together. We got in the car and drove in silence.

We had to park farther away from the theater than normal due to construction. Bright orange cones and signs directed us down a side alley between buildings as we walked to the theater. Still in silence.

My heart sighed. *Jesus, rescue this night.*

We turned a corner to a sign that read, *Construction Underway. Look Up.*

Five stories above, two steel beams were held by a crane. They were lit … and together formed the shape of a cross.

A few steps later, another sign. *Work in Process. Proceed with Care.*

Yep, I smiled. I needed patience. My son is a work in process.

I sensed Jesus smile back. *You both are.*

I gently put my arm on my son's shoulder. "I'm glad we're here. It's gonna be okay."

And we walked together, two works in process.

Even in Story 1, we're all unfinished works. So when you find yourself struggling with an issue you thought you'd overcome, it's helpful to view the process like steps on a spiral staircase.

Yep, you've already made one circle around this particular struggle. Maybe a few. That the issue is still present doesn't mean you're blowing it. Or that you'll never be free from it. You're not going in circles. You're just still on the journey. Each rotation on the spiral staircase takes you higher—with a new view of what's possible.

Whenever you feel stuck, pause to notice how far God has brought you. And remember his promises for even more as you follow him.

It's the kind of journey where you don't just arrive somewhere new. You arrive a new creation.

Times You're Unavailable

You weren't made to be in constant motion.

Being overly available at all times results in being overly exhausted at all times.

God has designed your soul to need regular times of restoration. That only occurs when you choose to be unavailable, at least for a moment, to the world's nonstop expectations.

But it is a choice that only you can make. And once you make it, you have to stick with it. Because you will be tested.

It's one thing to say you don't check texts or take calls after working hours. But when someone tries and you immediately respond, well, they know you weren't serious. And they'll keep doing it. Because your actions didn't match your words.

But the inverse is true as well. When you're consistently not being available during certain times, that becomes the norm.

Over time, you train others how to treat you by whether you choose to be overly available or to set healthy boundaries.

Take your Eden restoration seriously by telling the world when they can't reach you. And mean it.

Stand at the crossroads and look;
ask for the ancient paths,
ask where the good way is, and walk in it,
and you will find rest for your souls.

Jeremiah 6:16 NIV

Eden Beacon

Eating from the Tree of Life

After Adam and Eve ate from the wrong tree, they were banned from the garden. This act prevented them from then eating from the Tree of Life and living forever in their fallen state.

> And the LORD God said, "The man has now become like one of us, knowing good and evil. He must not be allowed to reach out his hand and take also from the tree of life and eat, and live forever." (Genesis 3:22 NIV)

The Tree of Life, the tree of all trees, was the central tree that the first man and woman were invited to eat from. Yet they passed on it. And it doesn't appear anyone has eaten from it since the world's first days.

But we will.

When we choose Jesus, we choose a different family tree. He becomes our Tree of Life. Our vine. And our way to the New Eden.

And in the New Eden, the Tree of Life awaits.

> Then the angel showed me the river of the water of life, as clear as crystal, flowing from the throne of God and of the Lamb down the middle of the great street of the city. On each side of the river stood the tree of life, bearing twelve crops of fruit, yielding its fruit every month. And the leaves of the tree are for the healing of the nations. No longer will there be any curse. (Revelation 22:1–3 NIV)

We get a taste now of what's to come. But one day we will eat from the Tree of Life.

What We Look to for Life

Here's another story that goes back to trees. This time one tree. But notice how the woodsman first uses it as a source for life (Tree of Life) but then begins to worship it rather than God (Tree of Knowledge).

The tale begins simply enough. A woodsman plants various trees in the forest, nurtures them, and, at the right time, chops one down for the raw material. He uses part of the wood to warm himself and bake his bread. His God-given gifting and skill have provided him a way to stay warm and be nourished. As Isaiah says,

> He cuts down cedars, he selects the cypress and the oak, he plants the ash in the forest to be nourished by the rain. And after his care, he uses part of the wood to make a fire to warm himself and bake his bread …

So far, so good. But then the artisan does something shocking. He takes the rest of the wood and begins to carve an idol for himself. He's no longer creating with God. He's trying to create his own personal god.

> … and then—he really does—he takes the rest of it and makes himself a god—a god for men to worship! An idol to fall down before and praise! Part of the tree he burns to roast his meat and to keep him warm and fed and well content, and with what's left he makes his god: a carved idol! He falls down before it and worships it and prays to it. "Deliver me," he says. "You are my god!" (Isaiah 44:14–17 TLB)

Notice it's the same person. Using the same gifting. On the same piece of wood. The only difference is, once he's well fed and warm, he turns his back on the Creator and places his hopes in his creation.

We tend to think we're too sophisticated for idols today. That's a lie. An idol is anything we give our hearts to in our search for life or success. We do this when we …

- worship our creativity more than our Creator;
- spend more time studying our craft than getting to know the One who gave us our creativity;

- look to the work of our hands, rather than to God, as the source that will deliver us.

We see these toxic traits play out in the sobering tale of the woodsman. It's what happens when our heart is divided, partially focused on God … and partially focused on making life work through our own strength.

I'll give Isaiah the last word:

> Such stupidity and ignorance! God has shut their eyes so that they cannot see and closed their minds from understanding. The man never stops to think or figure out, "Why, it's just a block of wood! I've burned it for heat and used it to bake my bread and roast my meat. How can the rest of it be a god? Should I fall down before a chunk of wood?" The poor, deluded fool feeds on ashes; he is trusting what can never give him any help at all. Yet he cannot bring himself to ask, "Is this thing, this idol that I'm holding in my hand, a lie?" (Isaiah 44:18–20 TLB)

It's a sobering tale of how easily we can fall back into Story 2 when we look to anything other than God for validation and life.

Our relationship with God is like a man who is
at home in his bed asleep. He dreams that
he is far away from home, and he is tired—
and he wishes he were at home in his bed asleep.

William J. Elliott, *Falling into the Face of God*

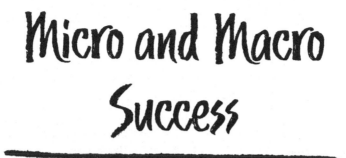 Micro and Macro Success

The world's applause will come and go. It may temporarily satisfy the ego, but never the soul.

Your deepest longings will never be satiated by a response from others ... or even by your own expectations. Real success simply comes down to this: did you pursue what you were doing with God?

Macro success occurs when you actively enter into your life and work with God. Doing so guarantees success because you experience success in each moment—not later depending on external reactions.

Let that sink in.

What you do with God is successful *before* anyone sees it. Even if no one sees it. The main focus is no longer how this Story 2 world rates you, but how you pursue your life and dreams.

Micro success may come in terms of money, applause, recognition, and status. But it is never guaranteed. These external aspects can be meaningful but were never meant to be the most meaningful part of your Story 1 life.

There really is no higher definition of success than pursuing all of life with God.

Start there and you'll live from a place of success rather than chasing after it. You'll also replace restless busyness with true Eden rest.

So don't you see that we don't owe this old do-it-yourself life one red cent. There's nothing in it for us, nothing at all. The best thing to do is give it a decent burial and get on with your new life. God's Spirit beckons. There are things to do and places to go!

Romans 8:12–14 MSG

Journey of Restoration

The Homeward Journey isn't meant to wear you out. It's meant to be a journey of restoration.

Being overly exhausted at the end of each day and looking for relief more than restoration are signs of a Story 2 life.

Eden rest is a necessary part of the Story 1 life. The goal isn't to make more happen. It's to go at God's pace in a world that has lost its rhythm.

The world sees rest as a way to simply recharge and do more. That's not how God sees it. Remember how God created, called it good, and rested? That's what we're after. Yet how often do we look back at what we spent time on, celebrate it, call it good, and rest?

If we constantly race from one event or need to the next—never building in time for rest—we'll end up weary and worn out. Soul care is essential.

We don't need you exhausted. We need you fully present. As a representative of Eden in this Story 2 world.

We get a taste of the New Eden as we restore our union, voice, vision, and rest. These are the four key traits of a Story 1 life.

Now, I want to offer you a glimpse of what awaits in the real country. The place that marks the end of the beginning and provides a first taste of forever.

We don't need you exhausted.
We need you fully present.
As a representative of Eden
in this Story 2 world.

The Real
Country

To die in one world is to be born into another.
Therefore life, like all created things,
though it ceases to flow in this world,
continues its journey in the place beyond.

Stephen R. Lawhead, *The Paradise War*

The Joyful Anticipation Deepens

There's a saying I've posted in my office with this simple encouragement:

Everything will be okay in the end. If it's not okay, it's not the end.

I'm not sure who first said this, but I like it. The words remind me that I live in a story, that God is the author, and that in spite of the turbulence of this particular page or chapter, it will ultimately end well.

Do the words sound overly optimistic to you? Too Pollyannaish? If so, I understand. But it is the prevailing worldview of Scripture. Listen to how Paul puts it:

That's why I don't think there's any comparison between the present hard times and the coming good times. The created world itself can hardly wait for what's coming next. Everything in creation is being more or less held back. God reins it in until both creation and all the creatures are ready and can be released at the same moment into the glorious times ahead. Meanwhile, the joyful anticipation deepens. (Romans 8:18–21 MSG)

Everything in creation anticipates this moment. It can hardly wait for what's coming next.

Let's do the same. The journey we're on isn't easy. The present times are hard.

But they don't hold a candle to the coming good times.

Eden Restored

The Homeward Journey isn't the quick or expedient path. Especially not in this Story 2 world.

But Story 1 allows us to reclaim so much of what was lost in Eden. Union with God. Our voice. Our vision. Our rest. As God intended it to be.

But a day is coming soon where we'll get Eden again. Not the original Eden. The New Eden.

We will walk again with God in the cool of the garden. Eat from the Tree of Life. Creation will be restored. Jesus will be King. All things will be made new. We will be fully seen, fully known, and fully loved. We will live in the city, the New Eden, with God at the epicenter.

We see the promise and the hope of this throughout Scripture.

Look! I am creating new heavens and a new earth, and no one will even think about the old ones anymore. Be glad; rejoice forever in my creation! (Isaiah 65:17–18 NLT)

I heard a loud shout from the throne, saying, "Look, God's home is now among his people! He will live with them, and they will be his people. God himself will be with them." (Revelation 21:3 NLT)

Then the angel showed me the river of the water of life, as clear as crystal, flowing from the throne of God and of the Lamb down the middle of the great street of the city. On each side of the river stood the tree of life, bearing twelve crops of fruit, yielding its fruit every month. And the leaves of the tree are for the healing of the nations. No longer will there be any curse. The throne of God and of the Lamb will be in the city, and his servants will serve him. They will see his face, and his name will be on their foreheads. There will be no more night. They will not need the light of a lamp or the light of the sun, for the Lord God will give them light. And they will reign for ever and ever. (Revelation 22:1–5 NIV)

And at that moment, we will experience far more than what the children of the fictional world of The Chronicles of Narnia did. A moment almost beyond words. The first taste of forever.

> But for them it was only the beginning of the real story. All their life in this world and all their adventures in Narnia had only been the cover and title page: now at last they were beginning Chapter One of the Great Story which no one on earth has read: which goes on forever: in which every chapter is better than the one before. (C. S. Lewis, *The Last Battle*)

And we will be able to say with the Unicorn,

> I have come home at last! This is my real country! I belong here. This is the land I have been looking for all my life, though I never knew it till now ... Come further up, come further in! (C. S. Lewis, *The Last Battle*)

"When I was small, not much bigger than a pollywog," said Frog, "my father said to me, 'Son, this is a cold, gray day but spring is just around the corner.' I wanted spring to come. I went out to find that corner.

"[After much searching], I was tired ... I went back home. When I got there, I found another corner. It was the corner of my house ... I saw birds sitting and singing in a tree. I saw my mother and father working in their garden ...

"I was very happy. I had found the corner that Spring was just around."

Arnold Lobel, *Frog and Toad All Year: The Corner*

It All Comes Down to This

The ultimate prize of the Homeward Journey isn't the Tree of Life or the New Eden. As good as they are, they are only good because God is good. Good creations can only come from a good Creator.

Our ultimate prize is God. He is the pearl of great price. In Eden, Adam and Eve traded intimacy with God for a self-led story. It was the worst deal in human history. Now, incredibly, we can trade it back for the true pearl. Life with God.

But to do so, we have to remember that the story of Eden isn't mostly about a home or creation or two trees or even Adam and Eve. It is a story about God's love. And nothing can separate us from that story or from his love.

> For I am persuaded that neither death nor life, nor angels nor principalities nor powers, nor things present nor things to come, nor height nor depth, nor any other created thing, shall be able to separate us from the love of God which is in Christ Jesus our Lord. (Romans 8:38–39 NKJV)

Adam and Eve received the same offer. The Tree of Life represented an intimate life together with God. Yet they looked to something else that held the illusion of greater life apart from God.

We can choose differently. We can pursue God with all of our heart, mind, soul, and strength. And we can be fully seen, known, and loved. And we will one day eat fruit from the Tree of Life.

> To him who overcomes I will give to eat from the tree of life, which is in the midst of the Paradise of God. (Revelation 2:7 NKJV)

But far better than that, we get God. In Paradise. That is everything.

We've focused on the two stories before us. God loves great stories. He created story. His favorites, however, aren't the ones we write, paint, or sing. They are the stories we're living.

May we live the kind of lives that future generations will tell as bedtime stories to inspire their children, to point them to a life wholly surrendered and fully lived with God.

Remember, there have always been two trees leading to two stories.

Story 1 or Story 2.

May we choose well.

This book is better because of the beautiful mix of your insights, encouragement, prayers, and wisdom.

I am beyond grateful.

Kellye Arnold, Greyson Arnold, Hope Arnold, Chase Arnold, Eric Burton, Karen Christakis, Lorie DeWorken, John Eldredge, Stasi Eldredge, Erin Healy, Nicole Howe, Amy Hudgens, Kristen Ingebretson, Gale Jones, Mindy Kiker, Jenny Kochert, Madeleine L'Engle, C. S. Lewis, Scott Morin, Jason Peet, Jeff Robinson, and Holly Varni

There Is More

Pursuing life and creativity with God is beautifully disruptive and immensely freeing. It begins with knowing God as both Creator and Father...and ourselves as his sons and daughters.

If you're tired of trying to get things done in your own strength or make success happen by following yet another formula, that's good. Because there is a better way. One that will awaken your heart...and your art.

As a fellow traveler, I hope you'll join me in that journey.

To discover more, visit withallen.com

**For free daily readings on God and Creativity, go to
withallen.com/sign-up**

About the Author

Allen Arnold is an author, speaker, and the Executive Producer of Content for Wild at Heart. His passion is awakening people's hearts to pursue their dreams and creativity with God. As a former fiction publisher, Allen oversaw the launch of more than 500 novels. Now he helps people live a better story. He loves blue oceans, black coffee, hot salsa, and big ideas. Discover more at **withallen.com**.

More Books by Allen

This isn't the end.

Just the end of Story 2.

And the beginning of Story 1.